what
WOMEN
want

marie claire

what
WOMEN
want

EDITED BY JACKIE FRANK

BANTAM BOOKS
SYDNEY • AUCKLAND • TORONTO • NEW YORK • LONDON

WHAT WOMEN WANT
A BANTAM BOOK

First published in Australia and New Zealand in 2002 by Bantam

National Library of Australia
Cataloguing-in-Publication Entry

What women want.

ISBN 1 86325 356 4.

1. Women – Australia. 2. Women – Australia – Social conditions. I. Frank, Jackie.

305.40994

Transworld Publishers,
a division of Random House Australia Pty Ltd
20 Alfred Street, Milsons Point, NSW 2061
http://www.randomhouse.com.au

Random House New Zealand Limited
18 Poland Road, Glenfield, Auckland

Transworld Publishers,
a division of The Random House Group Ltd
61-63 Uxbridge Road, London W5 5SA

Random House Inc
1540 Broadway, New York, New York 10036

Horton Hears a Who
™& © Dr. Seuss Enterprises, L.P. 1954.
All rights reserved. Used by permission.

Back cover photograph courtesy Herald Sun
Cover design by Adriana Cortazzo
Internal design by Midland Typesetters, Maryborough, Victoria
Typeset by Midland Typesetters, Maryborough, Victoria
Printed and bound by Griffin Press, Netley, South Australia

10 9 8 7 6 5 4 3 2 1

Contents

Contents

Contents

Foreword

Women are passionate about a whole range of issues. From the political to the personal, from global issues to matters that concern our families, from the economic realities of day-to-day life to the emotional realities of relationships, women want to be informed and we want to have a say. Most importantly, we want to make a difference.

Women are under a lot of pressure to be a certain type of person, to look a certain way, but at *marie claire* we celebrate the individual. Yes, women are interested in fashion and beauty, but at the same time we're interested in so much more. Women have enquiring minds and we want to know what's going on in the world around us. We want to know about women's lives in other parts of the world, and what they encounter and confront each and every day.

As individuals, women are powerful creatures. We know

we can do anything from running a household or running a business to running a country. But when women band together, as they have done for this book, we become even more powerful. We can do something about the world around us.

We know this from first-hand experience. Opportunities available to women in Australia have improved dramatically over the past century. But to get a feel for just how far we've come, we need to remember what things women 100 years ago said were most important to them.

They wanted basic improvement in health and sanitation, so that mothers and children didn't die in childbirth. They wanted the right to the same education as men. They wanted the right to enter male professions, which basically meant the workforce.

Consider this: before 1916, if a man died his widow did not have an automatic right to be legal guardian of their child. It wasn't until 1934 that women won equal custody rights. That such laws ever existed is now unthinkable.

We take all these things for granted today, but the battle has been hard fought.

Certainly the twentieth century was the century for women. It saw female prime ministers in countries like Sri Lanka, Britain, Israel, Turkey, Bangladesh and, closer to home, New Zealand. In Australia, during the 1970s and 1980s, the feminist movement pressured government into passing anti-discrimination laws. It also won funding for women's health centres, legal centres and rape-victim centres, as well as better childcare provisions.

In fact, Australian women led the way in many areas, starting in 1894 with the suffragettes who won women the right to vote in South Australia, long before women in America or Britain won that right. But we're still fighting for equality and progress in other areas. The principle of equal pay for equal work was adopted almost thirty years ago but we are yet to see it in practice: Australian women are currently earning around 80 cents to the male dollar. When it comes to maternity leave, Australia is the only Western country outside the United States that does not have paid maternity leave. The women of Algeria, Norway, England and Iraq, just to name a few, have it. So why don't we?

There's so much more to do. I started the What Women Want forums because I wanted to make *marie claire* magazine come alive. I also wanted to provide an umbrella under which women could unite and find their collective voice. What Women Want is about getting together to share views, ideas and passions. It's about having our say and taking action. And this book is just another way we can make a difference.

Each of the women in this book has written about a subject close to her heart, whether it's profoundly personal or an issue that affects each and every one of us. What unites them is that desire to make a difference, and a belief that when women get together anything is possible.

Jackie Frank
Sydney
August 2002

WENDY HARMER

Wendy Harmer has written numerous books and plays. Wendy has starred in and hosted a number of television shows and in 1993 joined the Sydney radio station 2Day FM's Morning Crew, which has rated number one on FM radio for the last ten years.

WENDY HARMER

Your Face is Your Fortune

When *marie claire* asked me late last year to nominate the topic I would speak about at the What Women Want forum I came up with the phrase 'Your face is your fortune' off the top of my head and then spent the next few months looking at these five words wondering why I had chosen them.

Of course there's no doubt your face COSTS you a fortune, and don't the skin care manufacturers' claims get more hilarious every year? I love the ad for a new cream which promises to 'attack ageing'. It says: 'Look three years younger in eight weeks or your money back.' I was thinking, what was so great about 1998 anyway? And big deal! I can look three years younger just by using the dimmer switch in the lounge. And I think the company's on a pretty safe bet with the 'or your money back' offer. Imagine going to consumer affairs to try to prove that you only look eighteen months younger, not three years.

Another product that caught my eye was the cream which promises to make your skin 54 per cent smoother and 71 per cent more radiant. How on earth are you supposed to measure radiance? Has someone invented a purse-pack radiometer? For example, 30 per cent radiance is like the light that comes out the back of the microwave; 50 per cent radiance is more like the interior light in a Volkswagen; and at 100 per cent radiance you can pluck your eyebrows without turning on the light in the bathroom.

I guess there's only one way to tell if you've used too much radiance cream: it's when your face is so radiant your husband dries his sports socks on your face. And you're really in trouble if he leaves you on a headland when he goes boating.

Yeah, so your face costs you a fortune, but is your face your fortune, as the old saying goes? As the weeks went by I started to realise that I had chosen this phrase, almost sub-consciously, because it represents a great conundrum to me. In one way I am living proof that these words are not true, and that's not just because these days I earn a good living working in radio. In another it's my face which has informed everything I do.

I was born forty-five years ago in a country town on a day that my father remembers as 'the best and the worst day' of his life. The best because his first-born child made her way into the world and the worst because he looked down to see a hole in her face where her nose and mouth should have been. I was born with a cleft palate and bilateral cleft lip and clearly, if my face was to be my fortune, I was heading for the dole queue.

These days when children in the Western world are born with a similar condition they are operated on quickly and can present an almost normal face to the world, but for me, back then, it was different. My face was patched together in a fairly rudimentary way and there was the promise that I lived with for all my childhood that one day I would have an operation which would make me look beautiful. But it couldn't happen until my head stopped growing. When would that be? No one could quite tell me for sure.

Over the years there were many expeditions from the country to Melbourne Children's Hospital, where I was photographed and examined, and I vividly remember asking my father: 'Has my head stopped growing yet, Dad?' And the answer would be: 'No, not yet. Maybe next year.'

The trip home in the back of the car would be a long and sorrowful one and then I would retreat to my room and look into the mirror and secretly imagine the beautiful face that one day would be mine and how my life would be transformed. I imagined a perfect face which would be admired, desired and loved by all. Wicked Witch Wendy would magically become Good Princess Wendy.

As it turned out I had my first operation when I was fourteen and the last when I was twenty-one. And the face I was left with is pretty much the one you see now. It functioned better, I could speak properly, it was not beautiful, not ugly, but unique and indelibly me.

And, of course, my life was not transformed, it just continued along as it always had. I wasn't loved any more or less, I wasn't any wiser and I wasn't any smarter. I was still

Wicked Witch Wendy, but I had the confidence to wear lipstick.

And in a way my face brings me here because it was the impetus for me to become a performer. I needed to present my imperfections to the world and say: 'I am no less a person because I look the way I do. I need you to look past the physical and recognise who I truly am.'

I am telling you my story in the light of a recent survey by an Australian women's magazine of 17 000 of its readers in which 70.2 per cent of them said they would have cosmetic surgery 'if money was no object'.

I find this statistic deeply disturbing. What does this survey say to me? It says that Australian women are living their lives waiting for the miracle of transformation. One day I will be beautiful! How many of us have hocked our lives to this fantasy? How many of us are missing out on all we could be, waiting for the day when we are finally revealed as Venus on the half-shell? As lean-limbed, full-lipped, flat-stomached beauties with smooth brows and full, high breasts?

How many of us believe that we are not good enough, no matter what our achievements? How many of us live every day with a more perfect imagined version of ourselves shadowing our every move, just slightly out of reach?

I am intrigued at the way this question was posed. Would the result have been the same if the question was: 'Would you have cosmetic surgery if pain was no object?' or 'Would you have cosmetic surgery if there was no guarantee, at all, that it would look any good?' And incidentally, I wonder whether the response would be the same if the question was: 'Would you like a BMW convertible if money was no object?'

In 1999 the New South Wales Health Department held an enquiry into cosmetic surgery. It found that the size of the industry had doubled in the past five years and that up to 200 000 surgical and cosmetic procedures were performed in Australia in 1998.

The report found that cosmetic surgery practitioners work outside the framework of organised medicine. There is no independent body to control the training and registration of cosmetic surgeons and no body to monitor the results for patients.

The report also found that the people who perform cosmetic surgery give no undertakings as to what they will do if something goes wrong and many of them operate in doctors' rooms where there is no regulation of safety and no reporting of complications.

Well, that's ironic isn't it? In other words, a $50 jar of face cream can offer guarantees, but spend $10 000 on a facelift and you're on your own!

And while the report acknowledges that 80 per cent of patients say they are happy with the results, it also says there's a problem with this statistic, because most of these responses are collected by the doctors themselves. How many women, in the face of their doctor, feel vain, foolish and ashamed to admit their procedure hasn't turned out the way they had hoped? How many of us can't even admit to our hairdressers we don't like our new hairdo? 'Oh, it's great,' we say and then we go home and cry in our bedrooms.

So if your surgery goes well, your doctor will take the credit; if it goes badly, you will be branded a neurotic woman with unreal expectations.

And leaving aside the fact that cosmetic surgery is way overpriced and many women go into debt to afford it, here's another statistic you might like to think about. Although we pay for breast implants ourselves in the first instance, any follow-up medical problems, like replacements or illness, are picked up by the taxpayer under Medicare. For every $1 out of our purse, it costs the public purse another $25.

It has been estimated that this has cost the taxpayer up to $500 million. This is money which could have been spent in hospitals. Is this what we want as women? How would you feel if your cosmetic surgery had prevented a hospital from buying a piece of medical equipment which could save a child's life?

And you might think, well, that's far-fetched, but while 6000 breast implants are put in every year, some 3000 are taken out or replaced. I'll bet we wouldn't tolerate that kind of failure rate on spare parts in the family car.

'Well, if it makes people feel better about themselves,' is the stock answer offered when anyone questions the cult of cosmetic surgery. And if you are constantly told that physical beauty will make you happier, then perhaps it will.

But it's almost as if the truism that 'beauty is only skin deep' has become an untruth. Beauty, we believe, makes us better people. It makes Elle Macpherson a good mother; it makes Nicole Kidman intelligent; it makes Cate Blanchett elegant, graceful and kind.

But what we know, but choose to forget, is that being beautiful doesn't make your kids love you any more; doesn't make you any more accomplished; doesn't make you friends. Physical beauty won't make your soul any more beautiful.

Do you ever remember as a child looking up at your nanna's deeply lined face and her crepey old skin draped like crushed velvet over the bones and thinking to yourself, 'If only Grandma could have a little work done, then I'd really love her'?

It's a case of the Emperor's New Clothes. We've all got friends who have, to use the euphemism, 'had a little work done'. Are you going to be the one to tell them that their eyes look a bit wonky, that their newly dermabraded skin looks plastic, that the Botox injections have taken away their character and left them with a mask you don't recognise any more? Or perhaps that their new breasts look hard and out of proportion with the rest of their body? Of course you aren't. You'll say, 'You look great,' and you'll be lying in response to their lie.

What is your friend saying to you when they have a facelift? Of course they'll tell you, 'I just wanted to look less tired,' but think about it. It's actually something quite profound. Your friend is saying: 'I do not want to grow old with you. I see you growing old before me and I am not coming with you. I will wipe our shared history from my face.'

They are also saying, in a way, that your friendship is not enough. 'All those cups of tea, the laughs, the shared secrets and the shoulder to cry on were not enough to sustain me. I need more to make me happy. And I need to go to a stranger, someone I have never met and may never meet again, who will put me through enormous physical pain to get it.'

And if you think about it, maybe if your friend really was ten years younger you may have never even met.

I'm asking you what can we offer to each other as women

that will take the place of this fantasy and heal this self-hatred? And forget blaming the media or the medical profession for this failure of confidence in ourselves, because, after all, both these institutions are our own creation. We can't blame men either. When you ask your partner whether you should have a nip and tuck, what does he say? 'But I love you just the way you are.' And that's exactly what you would say to him. Why is it any less believable coming from a man?

I want us to think how may our spirits, rather than our bodies, be transformed.

It must be unconditional love for each other, honesty, an uncritical eye. We have to re-learn to look past the physical body and to recognise the soul within.

We have to rediscover and redefine what we see as beautiful. Yes, a young and astonishingly beautiful face, a perfect, lithe body will always be a pleasure to see, but we have to remind ourselves that to watch a face ageing, to see the body sag and soften and give up its fight to take flight and slowly return to the earth from whence it came is also a deeply enriching experience.

I think we are seeing a failure of nerve by Australian women.

Are we finally standing at the doorway to independence and self-determination and we're too scared to walk through in case someone standing behind sees we have a fat bum?

Are we afraid to stand on a chair and smash the glass ceiling because someone might look up and see we've got a saggy neck?

We are asking the question: 'What do women want?'

Well, women have already said they want to be beautiful. Perhaps the question should be: 'What do women need?' I think that it's to be reminded that they are already beautiful.

This is an edited transcript of a speech Wendy gave at the *marie claire* What Women Want forum on 21 February 2001.

JULIE McCROSSIN

Julie McCrossin talks for a living. She is co-presenter with Geraldine Doogue of the national radio program 'Life Matters' on ABC Radio National. Previously she was a team leader for five years on the media quiz show 'Good News Week'. Julie has also worked as a TV reporter for both the Sydney Gay and Lesbian Mardi Gras and ANZAC Day – and she's proud to live in a country where such diversity is possible. Her proudest media moment was her appearance on 'Play School' as a silent clown called Plain Jane. Julie has university qualifications in the arts, education and law.

JULIE McCROSSIN

Learning Curves

While I was growing up, starting from when I was on the breast, my mother was saying, 'Get an education, get an education.' I'm going to show you a kind of family slide show that will illustrate where my mum's passion for education came from.

My mum is like countless other women: she believes that everyone should have the right to a decent education, regardless of their sex and no matter how much or how little their parents earn or where they live. But I fear that the right to an education, which I think is one of the great achievements of Australian democracy, is under threat, unless our politicians invest real money in public education.

(Just in case I forget, I want to pay tribute to the teachers I've had in both the public and the private systems. They were predominantly women and predominantly dedicated, and I think it's one of the great tragedies of our community that there aren't decent wages and better professional status for teachers.)

So I want to tell you the story of one woman whose passion for the idea that an education gives you more choices changed my life. So let me introduce you to my mum. My English mum (top photo, right). As you can see in the photo it's 1944. It's London, and it's just before she came out to Australia. She's in Trafalgar Square with the pigeons pooping on her like they've done on every one of us who's done the trip.

When my mum was thirteen she had to leave school and go to work. She was offered a scholarship to go to what the English called a grammar school. But my nanna, my mum's mum, was absolutely adamant that because they couldn't afford the uniform and the excursions and the other things that go with it all, her girl wasn't going to be embarrassed at school. And so my mum missed out on a high school education.

The next thing I want to show you is my parents on their wedding day (middle photo, right). It's the end of World War II. Women in Britain were called up during that war. So at eighteen my mum was called up and she was given a test and this test showed that she had above-average ability. My mum is in her late seventies now but she's still really proud of that bit of paper, because it's the one bit of objective evidence that she has of her educational capacity. I find it very, very moving when my mum talks about that test.

So as a result of her success in that test the British Women's Airforce gave her a job in signals on an air base and that's where she met one hell of a good-looking Aussie pilot. That was my dad (bottom photo, right). Check out the incredible six-pack – while we're talking about what women want.

Julie's mother Midge in Trafalgar Square, London – before travelling to Australia as a war bride on a ship of war brides.

The wedding day of Julie's mother Midge and father Bob – pictured centre, Bob's hands on Midge's shoulders – in Britain during World War II. Julie's mum was in the British Women's Airforce; her dad was in the Australian Airforce, a Pathfinder pilot.

Julie's father Bob.

My nanna was also called up and she became an ambulance driver, one of a pack of great babes in the middle of the London blitz (top photo, right). The bombs were falling and on their very first night out these women, many of them quite mature women, were taught to drive ambulances without the lights on. We're talking dead-set driving, girls, for anyone who's a driver. One night a bomb dropped on a building in Brixton and my nanna and her team of women had to pull forty dead and many injured people out of that rubble. These were ordinary women rising to the occasion because the men were at war.

Now, my nanna never went to school. She grew up on a farm and then the family moved in with a Baptist minister. My nanna always gave up drinking and smokes, but only for Lent. Whenever I travelled over to see her in Britain she'd say to me, 'Have you got the Black Label Johnny Walker duty free?' She had a Cockney accent and it always unnerved me because it was like I was living in 'Till Death Us Do Part', if anyone can remember that show.

But the only education my nanna got was from the Baptist minister at home. And after Nanna's war work was over, she had to work for money because my grandfather, who'd been driving trucks during the war, had a stroke. So she did the only thing she was qualified to do. She became a chauffeur. And so I grew up hearing about this rich lady called Miss Scarlet, who sounded incredibly alluring to a kid. Part of Nanna's job was to drive Miss Scarlet's dogs around in a car.

By the time I met her, Nanna was much older and by then she was a housekeeper for the Hove Police, just outside of Brighton in the south of England. She was a cleaning lady for the coppers until she was seventy-one years old.

Mrs Hedges, Julie's maternal grandmother, centre back row, with World War II London Blitz ambulance team. Julie's nanna was called up and spent her war service driving ambulances in London.

Julie, at front, with her mother Midge in 1956.

Julie showing a genetic tendency to have her hands on her hips – just like her mum in 1956.
(Courtesy Network Ten.)

Meanwhile, my mum had come out to Australia on a thing called a bride ship. Boatloads of women came out after the war. Then Mum had my two brothers and then me in 1954. Mum was English and worried about the sun so that rotten hat had to stay on my head (bottom-left photo, previous page). I had two sisters and two brothers, so Mum was busy. But what I want you to note is the stance of my mother. Note that physical position.

We now flash forward in time to a PR shot for 'Good News Week', the media quiz show (bottom-right photo, previous page). Ladies and gentlemen, you can see there's a genetic predisposition to this approach to life and it's a 'come and get me, here I am' kind of message.

(When I had my brief brush with television I learnt the incredible capacity of make-up to change how you look. I was a little disturbed that taxi drivers don't recognise me from the TV pictures. So I'd like to pay tribute now to the make-up women of television. Or, as my mate Amanda Keller calls it, the smash repairs.)

But anyway, the point of all this is that when my mum came out to Australia, the job she got was counting pennies for the Australian Post Office. I hope I'm not the only person old enough in this room to remember those things called pennies. For the younger girls and boys, they were big round coins and you put them in public telephones, and some poor buggers, and my mum was one of them, had to count the pennies to give them to the Post Office.

So my nanna and my mum were these gutsy, brave, bright women. And during the war there was Nanna driving ambulances in the London blitz and my mother in signals directing pilots where to go. And what are the jobs they can get after the war? Cleaning, driving and counting pennies. Now, I would not be true to the spirit of my mum and my nanna, who embody the Protestant work ethic as much as anyone on earth, if I didn't point out that they were proud and glad to have those jobs. I want to make that really clear.

But I guess another point is important too: these were the only choices Mum and Nanna had because they'd missed out on a good education. And so it's no wonder to me they were so determined that my brothers and sisters and I got a high school education. So here I am, my first day at school (top photo, next page). That cheesy grin was to stay there for the next fifty years of my life. You will notice that in any PR shot for television I've got the same bloody grin.

I was the first girl of the next generation to have the chance to get a high school education and to go on to uni. And of course Mum and Nanna were absolutely right: it did give me choices. But like any decent kid, I initially made none of the choices that my mum wanted. First of all, I chose to be a clown (middle photo, next page). Brian Joyce, a very strong man with a very good six-pack, is holding me upside down in this photo. I'm the head on the bottom. Of course, this is an unusual position for a children's entertainer, but it was good clean fun at the time.

I initially trained at university to be a primary school teacher but then I ran away, as you do, with the children's circus. I've still got that rather charming spotted dress, although I don't exactly fit in it any more! We did other more serious work in our theatre company. We went to prisons and juvenile justice institutions, as they're called – places we lock

First day at school.

Julie as a clown in Pipi Storm's children's circus with co-clown Brian Joyce, 1982.

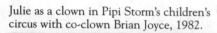

Julie as children's entertainer,
the unsuccessful rabbit.

up kids – and we put on performances about kids' legal rights – it was called legal education.

I worked with young children full-time for a year with Brian Joyce. And this was seriously the happiest and silliest part of my life. I really, really loved it. Although I was a tremendously unsuccessful rabbit (bottom photo, left).

Having graduated from university, I did what any decent Aussie girl would do. I chose to be a government bus driver because I'd always wanted to drive something big. I drove a New South Wales bus up and down the main street of Sydney for six months. Of course, my mother was keeling over by this stage and so were some of the passengers, because I had to have a pillow under my bottom to reach the pedals, which did not inspire confidence. But I can tell you my ambulance-driving nanna in Britain cheered when she heard the news because clearly driving was in the blood.

And then a bit later I met Paul McDermott – part man, part angel, part gorilla – and Mikey Robins, the fastest wit in the west (top photo, page 25). We worked together on 'Good News Week' for five years.

But during those years on 'Good News Week' I was off studying at uni, and I'm very pleased to say that I have now graduated with a law degree.

When I was trying on academic gowns I hoped to bring to my graduation just a hint of clown (middle photo, page 25). Wouldn't it be great if I was brave enough to wear the nose for the real thing, eh?

But my reason for being a part of What Women Want is because I got all these choices, to do silly things and big bus things and law things, because my mum and dad supported my getting an education. I mean, I tried to drop out and my mother dragged me by the hair back to that university, and any mother here who's got kids who are a bit flip-floppy will know what I'm saying. It takes a lot of parental support and particularly maternal support to keep a kid at uni.

And so I want to close by introducing you to one woman who I recently interviewed on my job on ABC Radio National. I'd like to introduce you to Stephanie Bugg. And this is a real person. Stephanie is seen here fixing a fridge (bottom photo, right). She won a gold medal for refrigeration mechanics at the International World Skills competition in Korea, the Olympics for apprentices, with thirty-five countries competing. Ladies and gentlemen, and the school kids here tonight – a special welcome to you – this is the Cathy Freeman of fridge mechanics.

Now, Stephanie Bugg has already travelled to Asia because she went and did that fridge mechanics course. She's now enrolled as an electrician. Stephanie Bugg may go to the moon. Why? Because Stephanie Bugg has got an education and anything is possible.

And so what do women want? I say women want what my mum never got: an opportunity for a decent education. I want a state school education to be as good as a private school education. And I want it not just because it's about individuals fulfilling their potential, particularly girls. (I mean, let's just think about the rotten Taliban: they wouldn't even let girls go to school.)

It's not just about individual potential. It's about being competitive in the world economy. We've got to have brain power and we want girls to do well in the twenty-first century. So it's funding for public education as well as private that I want.

Mikey Robins, Paul McDermott
and Julie on 'Good News Week'.
(Courtesy Network Ten.)

Julie graduated with a law
degree – minus the nose.

Stephanie Bugg competing at
the International World Skills
competition in Korea, 2001.
(Courtesy World Skills Australia.)

And I just want to close by thanking Mum. I want to thank her for pushing me and I want to thank Dad for supporting me. Here is my favourite photo of my mum and me as I'm falling into that cup of tea (photo below). Who doesn't want that degree of maternal approval beaming at them? And I want to thank them for the education that means I could be a lawyer – and a rabbit.

Julie and her mother in 1955.

This is an edited transcript of a speech Julie gave at the *marie claire* What Women Want forum on 10 October 2001.

BELINDA EMMETT

Belinda Emmett is one of Australia's favourite television stars. An accomplished singer and actor, she has been performing since the age of twelve. At nineteen Belinda was cast in the lead role of Tracy Russell in the sitcom 'Hey Dad'. She was soon offered a leading role in 'Home and Away', and her character, Rebecca, went on to become one of the most popular on television. Following a stint as presenter for 'Australia's All Time Favourite Bloopers', Belinda played Jodie in the television drama 'All Saints'. Recently she completed her first feature film alongside Eric Bana. *The Nugget* is due for release in 2002.

BELINDA EMMETT

Spirit

I think it's fairly common knowledge that at twenty-four I was diagnosed with breast cancer and have been in remission now for almost three years. So when I was asked to speak about something that I feel passionate about and having not yet been blessed with motherhood, I guess the cancer stood out as my most life-changing experience so far. Having survived it, it's obviously something that's close to my heart and I'm very passionate about raising funds for research so that one day my children or maybe grandchildren won't have to fear breast cancer, or any kind of cancer. That would be pretty incredible.

I can only speak from experience and I can only speak from the heart. I could rattle off facts and statistics, but I'm really no expert. I'm just some chick from the Central Coast who had it and survived it. But what I do know is that every four hours an Australian woman dies of breast cancer. It's the most lethal cancer for women in this country, and the sooner it's detected the better the chance of survival. A simple self-examination could save your life.

So if you ask me what I want, it's to raise awareness so that women realise that cancer doesn't discriminate. Not to live fearfully, but just to be aware. I want to educate women of all ages and stress the importance of early detection. Knowledge is a mighty weapon. I want to give support to those not fortunate enough to have support, both emotional and financial support. But essentially I want to be a living, breathing example of the fact that cancer need not be a death sentence. And that life after breast cancer can be really beautiful.

But the thing that I'm most passionate about is life. Not just life but really, really living. What I want is for all women to be able to live to their full potential, to be able to lead truly fulfilling lives. Because that's what really living is all about.

I'm treading a fine line here, I know. I don't want to sound preachy or like I've been saved and now I'm some saint who's skipping through the daisies. Because I'm definitely no saint and the world isn't always fair or good, and people aren't always fair or good, and there are a lot of things that unfortunately are not within our control.

But there are things that we can control. We can control our attitude and we can choose to believe in ourselves and the world and other people. Most people don't know what lies within them until they're forced to find it. If we did everything that we're capable of doing we would literally astound ourselves. I want women to be brave, be bold, speak up. If other people can make a difference with their ideas and actions, why can't you? There's nothing conceited in believing in the power that is within you.

When was the last time you did something that was really fulfilling? Something that made you remember what it's all about? We don't make time for those moments and yet they're the only ones that really count. Life is fleeting and it can be short. Make every day count.

Oh, and laugh a lot. I think there's humour to be found in just about anything. When I was diagnosed with breast cancer the boob jokes were flying thick and fast, and granted, I was the one who was making most of them but, believe me, it really, really helped. Life is too important to be taken too seriously.

I know this all sounds very romantic and idealistic, and although these words are coming from my mouth I don't always listen to them myself. I'm definitely a work in progress, but it's something to strive for.

Maybe in ten years' time my wants and passions will be a little more specific, but at the moment what I really want is to endeavour to live my life the best way I know how. And I want to encourage others to do the same.

This is an edited transcript of a speech Belinda gave at the *marie claire* What Women Want forum on 21 February 2001.

Postscript
It is now March 2002 and I'm two months out of a four-month chemotherapy stint after being diagnosed in September 2001 with secondary cancer in my bones.

On re-reading my speech I felt a sense of pride. Having not truly been tested in the way I feel I have this time around, the basic premise behind how I feel now and how I felt then is still the same. Life is wonderful and people are amazing. If only we'd all stop and realise that.

At twenty-seven my life so far has been an incredible journey. And although sometimes the challenges I've faced have seemed overwhelming, overcoming that feeling has given me enormous respect for and faith in the human spirit. Challenges can be empowering because they can give us the strength to have faith in ourselves and our own resources. Tapping into those resources leads to a whole new way of living. A way in which you listen to others and learn from them but are aware that the true answers lie within.

This may again sound unrealistic but I feel that it's something people need to understand and embrace, particularly when dealing with difficulties such as illness. Sometimes everything we've grown to rely on isn't so reliable and the world as we know it doesn't have the answers to our questions.

So, now, what do I want? Well, personally, to grow old and be happy. What do I want for women? I want women to believe that they have the power within themselves to do extraordinary things, and to live their lives in accordance with that belief.

JACKIE FRANK

Jackie Frank is the editor of *marie claire* Australia. She has worked on British *Elle* and British *marie claire*. Jackie helped launch the US edition of *marie claire* before returning to Australia in 1995 to take up the position of editor of the soon-to-be launched Australian *marie claire*. Most recently *marie claire* was awarded 2001 Magazine of the Year by the Magazine Publishers of Australia, as well as General Excellence – Lifestyle, Editorial Campaign of the Year and Best Use of Photography/Photographic Feature. Jackie is married with two children.

JACKIE FRANK

Not Being Perfectly Frank

The supermum. She's a myth, but I came up against her in the process of preparing this book. The publisher told me she'd had some anxious moments before our first appointment. She worried about what she would wear to a meeting with the editor of *marie claire* magazine. Surely, she thought, I would look immaculate. My make-up would be perfect, my hair freshly coiffed and my outfit straight out of the pages of last month's issue. I would certainly be a woman who had it all together, she reasoned.

Needless to say, when we did get together she was a bit surprised. I was, well, normal. Completely and utterly. My Vegemite-toast-on-the-run breakfast had seen to the last vestiges of lipstick, my hair was rolled up in a bun secured by a ballpoint pen and my outfit was whatever was clean and did not require ironing that morning as I rushed out after feeding, chasing and clothing my two adorable, wriggling toddlers.

Perfect? Not! Not at all, in fact. Just another Australian woman doing her best to keep all the balls in the air as she juggles a demanding job, two children under four and a marriage. My story is not unique. But via the What Women Want forums and this book, I hope to do my part to dispel the myth that there are mothers out there whose lives are simply perfect.

Let's face it: motherhood, while easier for some than for others, can be incredibly tough. So I want to shout from the rooftops that just coping with being a mother makes you a supermum.

Certainly, motherhood deserves more of society's respect and recognition. Because it's a tougher job than just about any other, from my experience. I launched *marie claire* magazine with very little knowledge of what was involved in that gargantuan task. And every month my team and I give birth to a new issue, which is no easy job. Bringing out a magazine involves long hours and lots of hard work. There are financial pressures, there are staff issues, and there are circulation targets to meet. But nothing – *nothing* – compares to the pressure, fear and sheer slog that goes into having and raising children.

And yet so many of us enter this alien world of motherhood with expectations that have but a fleeting acquaintance with reality. Sure, you will never know a love as deep and abiding as that you will have for your babies. You will never know such joy and nothing will ever be as fascinating as watching them develop into people with distinct personalities and characters. But you will also never know exhaustion, fear and guilt that cut you to the quick in quite the same way as when you're a mother.

There was a time when I subscribed to the supermum myth. During my first pregnancy it simply didn't enter my mind that I might have trouble coping. I might have the odd problem, I reasoned. But nothing that could not be fixed by a visit to the doctor or a hug from my husband.

My image of motherhood was pretty damned rosy. As long as my child was healthy, I would cope. I assumed that after he was born he would attach himself effortlessly to the breast then happily suck away ever so gently (in consideration of my nipples) at set times for however long I wished to breastfeed. And I fully expected that two weeks after my baby's birth I would be ready to leave him with a babysitter and set off for a romantic dinner *à deux* with my husband. Or, better still, I'd be all set to sparkle at a dinner party with baby sleeping contentedly in a cream wicker basket in the corner of the dining room. I imagined my baby would sleep enough for me to be able to read and walk and eat properly and do all the other things I like to do.

But as every mother knows, as soon as you become a parent all the best-laid plans are thrown out the window. The only certainty, as a grandmother recently told me, is that there won't be any. And while there are plenty of books about babies and parenting to devour before the birth, none of their advice really sinks in – and babies sure as hell don't read them!

Of course, I didn't seriously think that *everything* would be perfect. Even as a single woman my life was never that perfect. But until I had Charlie, my first baby, I had no idea just how far from reality my image of motherhood was.

I got my first inkling of the gap between rosy idealism and harsh reality when my husband and I attended prenatal classes. In our particular class there seemed a prevailing view that everything would go according to a plan, and there was pressure, I felt, to aim for a drug-free birth. Weeks later when I was in labour for real, my husband found it distressing when the female midwife – not the male doctor – questioned my need for painkillers early on because the contractions were exacerbating my existing chronic back problem. Of course, I was in too much agony to even think about being distressed.

Then once Charlie was born it was the breastfeeding. Our son just did not take to the breast. We tried everything, including 'tricking' him into sucking at the breast by expressing milk and feeding it through tubes attached to my nipples. Charlie cottoned on to that one immediately and just went straight for the tubes. I was desperate for help and feeling like such a failure because, as far as I knew, breastfeeding came completely naturally to every other mother. So why not me? Why couldn't I nourish my baby the way nature intended? It was such a struggle.

In my darkest hours I felt like I had fallen for an unspoken, unwritten conspiracy. And even now I believe that to be true. Because while I know there are plenty of mothers who have a dream run, my own experience and that of many women I have spoken with leads me to believe they are in the minority.

I firmly believe there are lots of women who don't tell, won't tell or simply refuse to believe the reality of their own life and so create a face, different to their own, which they can present to the world. I met a few of those women after I had Charlie. First they made me feel hopelessly inadequate. Later, I'm sorry to say, they made me feel angry. By pretending that everything is great and that they are effortlessly coping, women who portray their experiences as perfect deny each other the sort of honesty and support that would help lighten the burden that falls upon us when we try to be all things to all people.

Perhaps some women just (conveniently) forget. When Charlie was only a month old, friends asked us to dinner and I happily accepted. But when the afternoon of the dinner came around, I knew that getting out of the house was going to be impossible. I was physically and emotionally exhausted. Intelligent conversation would have been a stretch, but getting dressed and made up to face the world looking reasonably human was, on that day, a task that seemed beyond comprehension. So I phoned my friend and told her I was terribly sorry but we just weren't going to make it.

Rather than hearing the sort of understanding and sympathy I was expecting from someone who only a few years before had young children herself, I heard dismay coming down the phone line. My friend was upset I wasn't coming. 'Why?' she asked, as if having a terribly distressed, sobbing month-old baby was not enough. 'Why can't you make it?' She then suggested I just bring the baby in a basket and put him under the table.

I'm sure my friend did not mean for me to feel so belittled by the experience, but my nerves were raw and so was my response. After I'd put down the phone and turned to my husband, I was flabbergasted and incredulous that my friend seemed to have no memory of life with a newborn. But I also felt hugely inadequate. Shouldn't I be able to get dressed and leave the house for a dinner party? Is that what everyone else out there in new motherhood land was doing?

Apparently it was, if other people were to be believed. In

the meantime, I was exhausted. I looked a mess. And I was doing little to disguise it (the ever-present vomit on the shoulder was a dead give-away). I was making no attempt to hide how difficult I was finding my new life. Instead, I was out in the world saying, 'This is hell!' But when I talked to mothers outside my own circle – mothers I would meet at playgroup, the child health centre, or just walking in the park – it seemed I was the only one going through this.

There were some women who understood and were sympathetic, but there were many others who, it seemed to me, just didn't get it. Their babies slept through the night, sat peacefully in wicker baskets through dinner parties and fitted effortlessly into that elusive routine.

I couldn't believe that I was the only person feeling that way. So what was I doing wrong? Why was my baby crying so much and waking up all the time? The whole experience had the effect of undermining my self-esteem at a time when I needed it most. Because not enough people talk about how hard it is when things get tough – you can be completely knocked for six.

It was not until Charlie had cried for six hours straight one day that we discovered it was because he was hungry. Only then did I finally give in to the bottle. Later a doctor looked at Charlie's palate and asked immediately if I'd had trouble breastfeeding him. It turned out Charlie had an extremely high palate that would have made it virtually impossible for him to suck at the breast. If only I'd known earlier that breastfeeding does not come naturally to every woman so much stress could have been avoided, both by me and, most importantly, my baby.

By then I had started to come to grips with my own reality.

My expectations of motherhood had been so far from the truth I was experiencing as to be laughable. I admitted to myself that whether or not all these other perfect mothers needed help, I most certainly did. I spent time at the wonderful Karitane centre in Sydney's western suburbs to learn settling skills and get myself some much-needed rest. Back at home, my husband and I bit the bullet and hired mothercraft nurses. That is definitely a luxury that most families cannot afford, and certainly it hocked us, but it was something I needed for my survival and I wasn't ashamed to admit it.

We were fortunate to have an honest and open friend who'd had his first child six months before we did. Not long before Charlie was born, he had taken my husband aside and said, 'You know what? You think it's going to be the best thing that's ever happened to you, but it's a shocker.' He and his wife absolutely adored their child, of course, but because they were in the thick of it they could be honest with each other and with us.

It's this kind of honesty that's vital – between friends, women and especially partners. I can't imagine how difficult it must be for women whose partners are not supportive or with whom they don't have an honest relationship. Because your relationship with your partner is one extremely important part of life that changes irrevocably with the birth of a child. There is a shift in priorities, which I know some men are unable to deal with. I'm lucky to have a really supportive husband, but it is inevitable that in even the strongest partnerships the dynamics will change. Issues such as coming to grips with a single source of income, a woman's loss of libido, or even resentment of each other's role can be a source of friction.

Once again, talking it over with other women who are experiencing similar problems would be incredibly helpful. But still there is a reticence to discuss things that are so personal and yet so universal. Why? I can't even begin to imagine what it's like for single mums. Who do they turn to?

The best advice I could give to anyone embarking on motherhood or right in the thick of it is to simply refuse to feel like a failure, no matter what other mothers or experts are telling you. But this alone is no mean feat. I recall a particular paediatrician who treated me like an idiot. I had taken my son to him over a stomach problem and his first response was that I must have been doing something wrong with his formula feeding.

The answer to my baby's problem, as far as he was concerned, was to get me into the hospital so that I could make up a formula and then the doctors and nurses could see how I was doing it wrong! There I was, a successful magazine editor and businesswoman, and this man was telling me that I didn't know how to put seven scoops into 210 millilitres of water! So did I tell him where to put his theories? No. I was so massively sleep-deprived and strung out emotionally because I was worried about my child that I burst into tears and walked out of the surgery. And later I did what I was told and went into hospital and made up my baby's formula while the nurse looked on. Of course, I was mixing it correctly; in the end some drops prescribed by another doctor easily fixed Charlie's problem.

You need to be strong to be a new mother, because you really are at your most vulnerable. You also need to feel as good as possible about the decisions you make regarding working or staying at home. Neither is a walk in the park. For some mothers it is the hardest decision they will make; for others, working or staying at home is a no-brainer. For me, going back to work was part of my coping strategy. I needed to remind myself that I was a capable human being. For others, the choice to stay at home is made for reasons just as valid. Believing in your own decisions regarding your version of motherhood and respecting the choices and decisions that others make is an area in which we can all contribute.

In the end, however, you cannot escape the fact that motherhood is a wonderful, exhilarating adventure. And if women band together and refuse to believe the myth that it is always easy, and respect each other more, I believe we can make it more rewarding for all of us.

At *marie claire* recently, while researching an article on birth around the world, we found that in many cultures there is a forty-day period when the mother and baby are considered especially vulnerable and must be nurtured and cared for. In parts of China and India, the new mother stays in the family home and female relatives lovingly care for both her and the baby. In Nigeria, the baby's grandmother traditionally cares for mothers and babies in a special hut for two or three months before a feast is held in the mother's honour.

I'm not advocating we do the same, but these are examples of communities of women passing knowledge and support to each other. We can help ourselves ultimately by helping each other. Let's celebrate motherhood – in all its guises – together.

DEBORAH MAILMAN

Deborah Mailman grew up in Queensland's Mount Isa. In 1992 she graduated from Queensland University of Technology's Academy of the Arts. Since then Deb has worked extensively in theatre, film and television. Her films include *Dear Claudia*, *The Monkey's Mask*, *Rabbit Proof Fence* and *Radiance*, for which she received the AFI Best Actress Award and the Australian Film Critics Circle Award. Deb currently plays Kelly in Network Ten's 'The Secret Life of Us', for which she won the 2002 Silver Logie for Best Actress.

DEBORAH MAILMAN

Belles Letters

I *want to win an AFI award. I want to study at Boston's Commonwealth Shakespeare Company. I want to travel around my country in a ute.*

I wrote this letter to myself when I was seventeen.

> *I want to swim 2 ks every morning.*
> *I want good loving.*
> *I want to be fitter.*
> *I want recognition.*

I want to take time now to acknowledge the traditional owners of the land that we stand on, the Coolin Nation. I am a proud Bidjara woman, a Murri woman from Queensland, born and bred in Mount Isa, Kalkadoon country. I'd also like to acknowledge my Maori ancestry: Ngati Parou from the east coast of the north island, New Zealand.

I never set out wanting to change the world. All I wanted to be was an actor. And now I realise that is what acting is about: education, creating debate, helping to create understanding, stimulating the senses to allow people to look at the world we live in. That is my responsibility as an artist.

The difficulty that comes with that, and I think this is the case for a lot of Aboriginal achievers in the public eye, is I am sometimes called upon to be an authority on my culture. I'm asked questions about politics, and sometimes I get the sense that I'm expected to have answers or provide a solution. But I don't always have the knowledge to do so. So there is this enormous pressure to say the right thing. I'm learning right now that I can only speak on behalf of myself. But I'm proud that I am a positive role model, and I'm proud that I'm asked to speak about myself, my family, my sisters.

I just want to talk a little about Sisterhood. This Sisterhood, it's indefinable. It's when I'm with my sisters, my *tiddas*, and there's a familiarity of language that's verbal and non-verbal. It's the way we communicate that requires few words, and it gives us a sense of belonging. I love that we can talk like this. But one thing I want to say is, not all Aboriginal women, or all black women, want the same thing.

I have two sisters. One is an electrician by trade. She's a data-communications estimator in a male-dominated field and she is now dealing with motherhood for the first time. She just wants to get through the day. My other sister has left the work force. She's living on a farm.

I phoned up my mum the other day, and I said, 'Eh Mum, what do you want?'

'What do you mean, what do I want?' she said.

'What do you want?' I said.

'What do you mean, what do I want?'

'WHAT DO YOU WANT? If you could have anything now, what do you want?'

And she thought about it and she said: 'I want a garden.'

Of course, there are some fundamental community wants: better health systems, education systems that embrace cultural diversity, employment opportunities, maintaining language, keeping alive our stories, equal opportunities, respect, common courtesy, instilled pride in our children and our children's children. Those wants haven't shifted over time. And it is only thanks to the strength of the women and men that have gone before me that I am able to tell you fellas what I want.

But now, back to my letter. This is the updated version:

I want . . . the Swannies to win the premiership this year. I want longevity as an actor. I want to be a mother. I want an abundance of wealth. I want 'The Goodies' to return to the ABC. I want inner peace, world peace, Johnny Depp – a big piece. I want all school education to embrace diversity. I want a funky wedding with a chocolate crackle cake. I want to be proud of my achievements when I am old and grey. I want a matching bra and pants – I've never had that. I want siesta to become part of our working day. And I want to go home for the Mount Isa rodeo.

This is an edited transcript of a speech Deb gave at the *marie claire* What Women Want forum on 10 October 2001.

SALLY LOANE

Sally Loane has worked as a journalist in Australia and overseas for twenty-five years in radio, print and television. She is the presenter of the morning program on 702 ABC Sydney. Her first book, *Who Cares: Guilt, Hope and the Childcare Debate*, was published in 1997. She is married with two children.

SALLY LOANE

Losing John

A couple of days after my brother, John, died I dreamed about him. He was walking towards me, his handsome young face streaked with tears. In that paralysing, slow-motion fog that characterises a certain kind of dream, he could not speak, nor could I reach out to touch him. I woke up, desolate. Sixteen years later that dream is as vivid and disturbing as it was when I cried myself awake in the dead of a warm Brisbane night.

John killed himself. He organised his affairs, waved goodbye to Cindy, his long-time girlfriend who had gone away for the weekend, then sat down inside his home and took his life. He injected himself with a drug that vets use to put down animals. John was a veterinary surgeon, a pilot, twenty-eight years of age, six feet, six inches tall and engaged to be married. He left one short note, to Cindy, which explained nothing and everything. It stated: 'Everything that is mine, is now yours.' He signed it with his initials.

Everything on that terrible, terrible day in December sixteen years ago, when Cindy rang me to choke out her dreadful news, still stands out in stark relief over the blur of time and lapsed years. I remember the precise moment I took her call at my desk at work, and later, sitting on my verandah with my sister, Margie, as the darkness crawled over us, neither able to summon up the reserves to ring our mother.

Perhaps my most painful memory is seeing my father, a physically powerful but gentle giant of a man, born and bred on the land, racked with silent grief. Dad's eyes, hazel on an ordinary day, stood out bright emerald-green in rims reddened by weeping. I remember thinking that this was what my old university philosophy tutor meant when she said that grief distilled memory. She could always recall, she said, the exact colour and texture of her lover's tie as he spoke the words (long forgotten) that ended their relationship. I remember the brilliant green of my father's eyes the week my brother died.

How can one explain the agony a suicide causes a family? The cluster bomb of despair that is detonated. The nagging worry that we suspected something was amiss and failed to act. The phone calls we put off, the contact we neglected. Was I too bossy an older sister to this sensitive little boy born two years after me? Was there something I'd done or said during our growing-up years to damage him? I kept thinking about John's first day at primary school, when he wet his pants in fear. Was I sympathetic and caring or did I walk away in hot shame, leaving him to wilt under the stares of the older kids? I can never remember.

We were very different, John and I. We fought a bit as teenagers – he the annoying little brother with a wicked sense of humour, me the classic older sister, serious and responsible, possessed of a finely honed and devastating verbal put-down. And yet, when I gaze at the photos our parents took of us – me, John and our baby sister, Margie – I knew I had loved him dearly. There we are, splashing around in a water-filled galvanised iron tub in our garden, our version of a backyard pool on the family's 2000-hectare wool property in northern New South Wales. Mum's camera caught us, beautifully dressed in the smocked and shirred cottons of the 1960s, grinning, happy. I often have my arm around him. He was a dear, lovable little boy, dimpled, always laughing. He used to cart a battered and empty Saxa salt canister around with him, sucking away at the traces of salt. He also sucked his thumb, something Mum was always trying to cure. He was soft hearted, and would cry at the memory of some sad story Mum had read him – Hansel and Gretel or Bambi or Dumbo, the little elephant who was teased for his giant ears.

We were sent away to the city to boarding schools: me first, then John and later Margie. When we returned home in the holidays we instantly resumed our lives as country kids. John was most at home on the back of a motorbike, or tinkering away with an old clock, or repairing something electronic. He was clever with his hands, like Dad, and possessed a formidable intelligence.

At school and university John's best subjects were physics, chemistry and maths. He did well in exams, sailing through the weeks of study. He had a passion for computers in the days when only scientists and a small group of aficionados had a clue what they were about. He spent hours reading specialist computer and electronics magazines. He was a talented sportsman too, excelling in athletics, rugby and rowing. He and his oldest and closest school and uni mate, Tim, rowed for the first eight in the Head of the River and also in the fours, going on to compete in the state championships.

John was a regular uni student, happiest in moleskins at a backyard barbecue with friends, beer and cigarette in hand. He met his beloved Cindy at vet school. She was tiny and blonde, the exact physical opposite to his mother and sisters.

I was the last one in John's immediate family to see him before he died. In August 1986 I was in north Queensland with a friend and colleague from the *National Times on Sunday*, photographer Lorrie Graham. Lorrie and I were on the road, looking for stories, and we spent a night in Mount Isa, where John and Cindy lived. We were passing through en route from Darwin, where we'd been covering the Royal Commission of Inquiry into Lindy Chamberlain's conviction, and were heading towards Karumba in the Gulf of Carpentaria.

John and Cindy lived in Mount Isa so John could pursue the vet work he loved, flying around station properties to do cattle work. John adored the outback. One of his first jobs when he graduated had been at Kununurra in the Northern Territory, where he worked as a flying vet for the country's original flying vet, David Bradley. My sister's favourite photo of John is one of him standing near his plane after a day's work, in his riding boots and bushie's shirt, grinning fit to burst.

I was shocked when I saw John that August. He had put on a lot of weight and seemed unnaturally quiet and reserved. He'd always had something of a temper, even as a teenager, swinging from volatility to sunshine in a short space of time. This time there was none of that. His mood was evenly flat and down. Even allowing for the day's blistering heat he spent a great deal of time sleeping. The laconic, funny, smart, quick-tempered brother I'd known had all but disappeared.

Mount Isa I had hated on sight. Godforsaken, grimy and isolated, it hunkered down under the merciless sun like a reptile on a rock. There was a sullen menace I couldn't put my finger on. It depressed me like no other place I'd ever encountered. Or did I imagine all this in hindsight when I thought about my kid brother lying on his kitchen floor, alone? Did I have a nagging, prickling feeling that, back then in August, four months before he died, he had taken himself to some sort of nameless, lonely place I couldn't identify? I don't know. I just knew he wasn't right and I had no idea what was wrong.

My first thoughts were that it might have been the town and the relentless tropical summer that was getting him down. It certainly depressed me. I knew enough about north Queensland and its unforgiving climate to know that people went mad in that heat. My second thoughts were that it could have been his job. He spent long periods of time in some of the most isolated places in the country, testing cattle for tuberculosis and brucellosis on remote properties. He camped out, often with Aboriginal stockmen. He'd told me on one occasion that he often didn't talk to another white man for weeks. When we spoke about that, the Christmas the year before he died, I remember thinking that he had changed, that he had become quieter and more withdrawn. It was hard to draw him out in conversation.

Should I have said something, rung around the family, got us all together to see if we all had the same worries? In hindsight, of course I should have. At the time, though, life and its relentless pace got in the way. You tamp down stuff like that in the back of your mind and tell yourself to stop worrying. Things will be okay.

My mother was also concerned about the changes she observed in her son that Christmas, eleven months before he died. He was restless and at times uncommunicative. If any of us in the family tried to draw him out or to broach the subject of his health and wellbeing, John drew a curtain over the issue. It was as though his personality had slipped off the dial a little, like a poorly tuned radio. There was nothing tangible, like a broken limb or a chronic cough, that we could bundle up and take to the doctor's surgery.

We said goodbye to John on a brilliant sunny day in our home town in the verdant high country of the New England tableland. The clan gathered in the Presbyterian church and the minister who'd christened John, an old family friend, solemnly conducted the memorial service. I can't remember ever feeling so sad, watching my poor mother and father and my stepmother, Barbie, who'd known and loved John for most of his life, try to get through the service. I felt no peace, as one is probably supposed to, only the physical pain of being unable to stop sobbing in great heaving waves.

My extended family looks as though we've all been carved from the same block of granite: country people, generations of graziers, wiry, tweed-jacketed descendants of Scottish and English settlers. I'd grown up with my cousins, some of us becoming almost as close as siblings when we were kids. I have some sweet photos of all of us when we were tiny, taken at the polocrosse games we went to with our parents when they played against teams from surrounding districts. We're all standing in line, holding hands, giggling, little girls in plaits, the boys in cut-down jodhpurs. Two decades later we were all adults. Some of us had gone away to uni, some had come back to work on the family properties, some had married and had children of their own.

The sense of loss and sadness as we gathered in a family friend's big shady garden for lunch after the service was almost unbearable. There was so little to grasp on to, as people do in times of bereavement. John had not died in a tragic accident, crashed his plane or his car in the great outback spaces where he worked. He had taken his own life. Our family hadn't experienced suicide before. We had no words for it, no explanations.

So, why, John, why? In the weeks after he died, when we were flattened with grief and preoccupied with the mundane business of death – organising the funeral, sorting out the legal and medical requirements, tidying up the stuff John had accumulated in his short life and, finally, trying to get through Christmas – none of us had much of a clue. With hindsight, I am now able to say that when I'd seen John in Mount Isa three and a half months before he died he had been deeply depressed. Now I know more about the condition Winston Churchill described as the 'black dog' I recognise the symptoms John had – sleeping during the day, an unwillingness to communicate, weight gain – as being those of depression.

Or was it? My father had other suspicions, the chief one being that John had Ross River virus, a mosquito-borne disease that can have dreadful effects on sufferers, including depression. Many people in rural Australia, particularly in the north, where there is a lot of Ross River virus, have reported devastating psychological symptoms in family members who have had it.

Back then, I thought John was going through a rough patch. There were problems with his vet work and his employers, problems that seemed to be getting on top of him and causing him to lose perspective on things that normally would not have fazed him too much. Surely it would pass, surely he would re-rail his life. John was a young man who had never been anything but a huge achiever, intellectually and physically. As well, he and Cindy were engaged to be married, and they were both coming home for Christmas.

But there *was* something else. Something very serious that would eventually lead us all to similar conclusions about how our John stepped into the heart of darkness and never came out.

That something was a parasitic disease called toxoplasmosis. John contracted toxoplasmosis, colloquially called toxo, while he was at university. Humans get it either from eating raw or partially cooked meat containing the parasite *Toxoplasma gondii* or they ingest it accidentally via contaminated cat faeces. John was convinced he got toxo from a sick cat he was treating in the vet school's animal hospital. While the disease is relatively common – in some countries it's estimated that up to 60 per cent of the population have it – in most people it lies dormant, with few or no symptoms for the rest of their lives. But in rare cases it can be devastating. At the height of the disease the highly infectious and resistant toxoplasma oocyte moves through the bloodstream and embeds itself in various organs and muscle tissues. If women contract it while pregnant it can inflict gross abnormalities on their unborn babies, including vision and hearing problems and mental retardation.

Despite the fact that John was a supremely fit and healthy young man, toxoplasmosis made him gravely ill, with severe flu-like symptoms and extreme fatigue. At first the doctors couldn't diagnose what was wrong. It was John, the fourth-year vet student with a great deal of knowledge about animal diseases that cross into humans, who told them to try testing for toxoplasmosis. The disease affected him so badly he had to take a whole year off uni to recover.

Is this when we started to see changes in his mood? My sister, Margie, recalls that John did a lot of lying around, sleeping and reading his computer magazines. Our mother can pinpoint the changes in his moods from the year he got toxoplasmosis, but for many years it was not very noticeable. He recovered, went back to uni and completed vet science with flying colours, finishing in the top five in his year.

After graduating in 1981, John set out on the big adventure of a career in his beloved veterinary science – and it wasn't going to be with small, fluffy household pets. John loved the bush and big animal work. His first job after graduating was to work in a vet practice in Charters Towers in Queensland – cattle country. He decided to strike out on his own as a vet, and went further afield, to Kununurra in Western Australia, working on the Bradleys' vast cattle station there. Up there, light planes were used to cover the huge distances, so John went back east and got his pilot's licence. The flying school operators said he was one of the best and brightest pupils they'd ever had. He and Cindy, together since uni, eventually moved to Mount Isa to set up home and make it their base for big animal vet work.

Three years after John contracted toxoplasmosis, he began to experience problems in one of his eyes. An ophthalmologist delivered the bad news – it was a lesion caused by the toxoplasmosis parasite. The prognosis was not good. He could lose the sight in his eye, which would of course prevent him from flying planes. John was devastated by the news, but would not talk to his family about it. At about the same time he also began to suffer bouts of what we now know was depression.

Perhaps the most terrifying and little-known aspect of toxo-plasmosis is that it affects the brain and can cause headaches and personality and mood changes, including depression and social withdrawal. Until relatively recently, there has been scant detailed research on the effects of toxoplasmosis in humans, but it has come to prominence in medical research because HIV/AIDS patients with suppressed immune systems are highly susceptible to toxoplasmosis infections and can become severely ill.

To try to understand how it affects the human brain, researchers have looked at what happens to a rat or a mouse which hosts the parasite. When a mouse has toxoplasmosis, it affects the brain's neurotransmitters, so that the mouse does not recognise the smell of cat urine, rendering it immune to its natural fear of cats. The cat is able therefore to kill the affected and infected mouse, and so the parasite is passed on to its next host, the cat.

Using this information, researchers at the Charles Univer-sity in Prague have been conducting personality tests on people with latent toxoplasmosis, and have found there are noticeable changes. In some people with acute toxoplasmosis infections, there are case reports of more severe psychiatric and behavioural abnormalities.

Our family has absolutely no doubt that John's severe toxo-plasmosis infection started a chain of events and changes in his brain which led to his acute depressive state and then to his suicide. We know that this intelligent young man read everything he could get his hands on about the disease and, despite the paucity of research at the time, was left in no doubt that the prognosis for his eyesight and his physical and mental capacities could be very poor indeed. Was this knowledge enough to trigger depression, or was it a toxoplasmosis lesion in his brain which caused depression? These are questions that will always remain unanswered. We were not armed with enough knowledge to ask the doctors for a detailed post-mortem, which may have shed some light on what it was that led to John's premature death.

It's hard to ever stop thinking of what might have been – what might have been if I'd alerted a doctor or mobilised someone else in the family to get John to medical help. Would there have been a drug that could have lifted his depression? Was there treatment to treat the toxoplasmosis lesions and reverse their effects on his body? The passing years might ease the pain of losing John, but the 'what ifs' never fade.

The slivers of memory I hold dearest of my brother, John, are the simplest ones, of the time when I knew him best – our childhood. The time when we spent every moment of the day for a week building a road and freeway system from the back steps to the dam in the home paddock for our toy trucks and cars; when the two of us camped in the paddock for the first time and woke in fright at the sound of grazing horses outside our tent; the mornings when he cajoled me into joining him on his frosty dawn run to check his rabbit traps; the idyllic days when we walked to the main road together to catch the school bus, pausing to crack the ice on top of the small dam near the gate in winter, to catch tadpoles in summer.

A tree, planted for John's memory, flourishes sturdy and strong in the garden of the family property, which our grandfather settled in the early 1900s. It is the same garden in which John played as a little boy in cotton dungarees, sucking on his old salt can, pushing a toy grader through the dirt.

John was his parents' only son, the boy they called (after AA Milne) 'Jonathan Joe with a mouth like an O and a wheelbarrow full of surprises'.

He was my brother. He grew to be a fine boy and a fine man. I want nothing more than to know that he found some kind of peace and happiness again.

In memory, John Douglas Fraser, 9 April 1958 – 10 December 1986

KATE DUTHIE

Kate Duthie is a journalist at *The Sydney Morning Herald,* where she edits *The Guide* and writes the bar reviews in *Good Living.*

Photograph: Jennifer Soo

KATE DUTHIE

Thanks for the Mammaries

B*reasts, hooters, norks, bristols, bazookers, tits, bazoombas, jugs, love pillows, baps, knockers, rack, mams, milk machines, boobs.*

– Anon

Unluckily for me, since puberty I have had a predisposition towards the larger end of the breast market, making my bust a dominant force in my life.

In my teens I decided they were the 'correct' size, allowing me to keep boys interested without being deemed freakish. By my late twenties I fitted nicely into a D cup, but I always felt I was a bit too big. Okay, so I didn't need to go to a special bra shop and be fitted by ladies with metres of tape measure, industrial cabling and mouths full of nails. And I never had to leaf through special mail-order brochures for the stout-chested E, F and G cuppers, but my D-cup fillers had a way of messing things up. They had a tendency to stretch a T-shirt logo into an illegibly elastic smear. They were capable of ruining my dream Hepburn-style gown by appearing, uninvited, as a steaming pair of puds over the top of the tightly boned corset. Most memorably, they regularly wrestled their way out, both over the top and under the wire, of my bras, in a vain bid for freedom, creating a pair of double breasts in the process.

It's not my fault. I come from a long line of large-breasted women. Huge enormous breasts all of them. In my family, if you don't have a couple of bouncing, plump, aubergine-like attachments in your bra you're a man. My grandmothers were both blessed with prominent mammaries. I recall their enormous Ambrose Wilson corsetry items flapping menacingly on the washing line, blocking out the sun on the best day of summer, or, when dried on a heater, smothering the warmth on a winter's night. To me, it was a haunting glimpse of what lay ahead. My mum and her sister, Eileen, carried on the busty family trend and between them produced three daughters who also bore the terrible legacy of the dangerously stretched button-up blouse.

All this bosom-related fun changed shortly after I turned thirty and was diagnosed with breast cancer. Within days of discovering the lump I was in hospital being operated on. A lumpectomy and the removal of lymph nodes led to the discovery of two further pre-cancerous areas in my right breast and that the cancer had already spread to my lymphatic system. Within the week I had had a mastectomy, my breast replaced by a long, thick red scar. Later that month I started a gruelling six-month regime of chemotherapy that would leave me sick, bald and fat.

Eighteen months ago I took the preventative measure of having my other breast removed, followed by a massive operation to reconstruct both breasts. Not a barrel of laughs at all. The upside is my bra-wearing days are over. No more ugly red welts in my shoulders. No more ruined T-shirt logos. Just two perky pups standing proud.

In the whole time I was going through the illness and treatment no one was ever able to show me a book or magazine article containing the faintest glimpse of humour. Books with titles like *Before I Cark It* and *Is She Dead Yet?* seemed to be *de rigeur* when it came to uplifting breast cancer tomes. But through all the bad times there were flashes of bright laughter and surprisingly joyful and amazing moments, none of which I would have experienced if I hadn't had breast cancer.

What I wanted then and what I want for all women now is to know that if you have breast cancer or any other serious disease you have to decide whether you are going to let it run and ruin your life or whether you are going to accept it as just another step along the road and treat it as the unique experience it is. Yes, it's serious stuff. It's terrifying and lonely and bleak and all the other things you think it would be. But it's also a lot of things you wouldn't expect. I chose to deal with my fear and loss by finding all the good stuff I could, no matter how small. The stuff that made me laugh till I thought my stitches would burst, or the happy days with my husband when he said all the right things, or the ways in which my friends revealed their love for us. It's all good stuff.

So instead of banging on about all the sad bits you've read a million times before, I want to use this essay as a way of highlighting the good times. Here, then, is my homage to my much-missed breasts and a glimpse into the joyful, uplifting world of breast cancer. A walk down mammary lane, if you will.

What women want – non-squash mammograms

Now, I don't want to put anyone off getting a mammogram because they are life savers, literally, but I mean, honestly, I hope one day there will be a better way of checking a breast for tumours other than squashing it flat enough to slide under a door.

The experience of the mammogram was completely alien to me. No sooner had my robe fallen to the floor than the mammographer had my breast pummelled flat and jammed between two flat plastic plates, which she squeezed tighter and tighter with every touch of her foot pedal. She had tiny hands which she used to twist and turn my relatively gargantuan breast as if wringing out a towel. Did she not see it was still attached to my body and that was just the way I liked it? When my body part had been turned into pizza dough I was quite prepared to see it generously covered in tomato sauce and mozzarella and shoved into a wood-fired oven. The relief I felt when my breast sprung free at the release of the plastic mangle was memorable.

Gotta love those mammograms though. The results showed my tumour was serious enough to warrant further investigation and I was packed off to a breast surgeon.

What women want – sensitive doctors

My surgeon was fantastic, don't get me wrong, but having seen thousands of breasts in his forty-odd years as a breast surgeon he was a little blasé about them.

My initial visit to his office was the first of many encounters with strange men who thought nothing of having a good old rummage around my bosoms, discussing cancer in an almost casual way while asking me if I had any plans to go away on holiday.

'Yes, we thought Thailand – oh, apart from the fact that I've just been diagnosed with cancer and will probably be busy having painful surgery and undergoing horrendous chemotherapy. How about you? I hear that Fiji is super at this time of year.'

Also, as he was a rather old-fashioned sort of man he always addressed me as 'Mrs Duthie', as if we were at a church morning tea, even though he was cupping my breast and giving it a right old squeeze at the time.

When in hospital awaiting surgery he would regularly pop into my cubicle with his registrar and intern. After pulling the curtain around, the three of them would go to town with the old breast, juggling, almost as if they hadn't noticed I was there. Funny sods those doctors.

What women want – husbands like mine

I'd like to say a bit about my amazing and fantastic husband, Rob. All women deserve him but they can't have him. He's mine. He positively shone during my cancer and treatment. You know how men always say the wrong thing and never ever understand that even when asked, 'Does my bum look big in this?' every day, the answer is always no? When I was sick Rob got it right every time.

We have always felt like two halves of a whole, so when I was diagnosed Rob was just as scared and upset as I was. There's nothing like a good case of cancer to bring you even closer together, let me tell you. I had heard horror stories about husbands rejecting their wives after mastectomy surgery and even punching their wives' scars, so I wasn't sure how we would cope with my disfigured body.

While it has taken me years to come to terms with my appearance, Rob was amazing about it from the start. When I woke after my mastectomy the pain felt like a bus was parked on my chest. The first thing I did was lift the sheet and look down at the flat bit where my breast had been. Blimey.

When I got back up to the ward, Rob was waiting for me. 'Well, we better have a look at this then,' I said, and I lifted the sheet for Rob to see.

He had a good look. 'Well, I think you're even more beautiful now than you were before,' he said.

I can't imagine him having said anything better. I have never forgotten how great it made me feel and how much I loved him at that moment.

I was in hospital for two weeks but Rob came to the ward every day and sat with me from the moment visiting hours began to when they threw him out. And when I was sent home still attached to a drainage tube and had trouble bathing, dressing and moving around, he helped me with it all. A round of applause, please, for my husband.

What women want – great painkilling drugs

But not the ones that make you talk rubbish. One of the wonders of modern science is the painkiller. Gotta love that morphine when you wake from five hours on the slab. And pethidine deserves a quick mention too: it gives you a fabulous giggly high without getting the cops involved.

But for me the biggest problem with major surgery, apart from the way a general anaesthetic messes with your body and your head, is that often anaesthetists want to give you drugs to 'relax' you before surgery. Now, you might quite like the idea of being a bit chilled before going under the knife but just a sniff of those drugs turns me into a babbling idiot. Sure, I'm relaxed and happy, but I talk even more rubbish than usual. The worst bit is that all the time I'm jabbering on like a demented monkey woman I am completely aware of what utter cack is spilling from my lips but have no control over it.

A few months ago, about eight months after my last major surgery, I had a small follow-up op. I told my surgeon I didn't want a premed drug as I suspected it might make me talk rubbish and I wondered if he had noticed. He laughed. A lot, actually, and then told me that he and his team still enjoyed a good laugh recalling my babbling before the operation eight months previously. Apparently I suggested to the whole gowned-up operating team that we all meet up and have dinner straight after the op. It was all they could do to get the anaesthetic in me to knock me out and shut me up.

What women want – hospital girlfriends

I spent two weeks in a hospital ward of four women, so I went from being the new girl to the sort of ward madam. Patients came and went and I got to know most of them. They were all lovely women, apart from an old Italian woman who made a great deal of noise in the lav. For the short time we knew each other there was a great bond as we shared good and bad health news.

My favourite bit was the sort of unspoken patient competitiveness. Who had what. How many stitches they'd had. How many nights they'd be in. 'Oh, so just an appendicitis eh? Me? Oh yeah, breast cancer. Yeah that's right, a mastectomy.

Oh yeah, fifty staples in my chest. Oh, is that your scar? I could hardly see it. Beryl over there's in for her fifth op in two years. Bowel stuff. Now she's in A LOT of pain so you might want to keep your whining to a minimum.' Loved that.

We helped each other manage pain with a good laugh, and comforted each other when we got bad news. The curtains separating us from each other didn't allow for much privacy so everyone could hear what our doctors were saying. Rob was with me when we were told I would have to have a mastectomy, but in the evening when he had gone I was left to cry alone. A young woman in the bed across from me came and sat with me and held my hand while I cried. I loved that.

My ward soul mate was Lorraine. She suffered from Crohn's disease, an agonising bowel disorder that required regular and painful abdominal surgery. She was in pain a lot of the time but we laughed every day, mainly at her necessary but agonising attempts to squeeze out even the tiniest bit of wind. She would get on all fours, desperate to relieve the pressure build-up in her bowel. While the rest of us shouted words of encouragement she would clench everything and push. The silence would be broken by the tiniest squeak followed by peals of laughter and then cries of pain as we gripped our own broken bodies. By the time each woman left we knew each other's husband, children's names and holiday plans. I remember it as a happy time.

What women want – great-shaped heads

Oh yes. The joys of chemotherapy. I hated chemotherapy with a passion, and without a doubt for me it was the worst part of the whole experience. I like to think I'm great mates with my oncologist and I got to know all the chemo nurses and the other patients being treated, but I hated it. The hours spent sitting in a room full of other sick people wondering who might make it and who we would lose, watching each other suffer, watching the hair disappear week after week, feeling the searing pain of the canular being inserted into weaker and weaker veins in the back of my hand, the sickness, the tiredness, the bloating, the weight gain, the depression.

This was the hardest part of the experience in which to find the joy, the fun and the laughter. But I did. In the baldness.

We knew my hair would fall out about twelve days after my first dose of chemo. So Rob took a few photos of me for the album and then I went to the hairdresser and had my hair cropped. When my hair started coming out in handfuls at least they were only small ones. A few days later Rob shaved off the odd hairs that were left and shaved his own head, too.

It turned out I had a pretty well-shaped head and, as it was summer, it wasn't long before it was golden brown. We lived in Glebe then, which is a great place to live if you don't want to stand out. Glebe is the home of Sydney's card-carrying, New Age, crystal-hugging, chakra-loving, shoeless-children, dogs-on-ropes hippies. A place where a woman with a bald head doesn't attract even a second glance. When it came to my shiny pate, most people admired it, some wanted to emulate it and everyone wanted to touch it. For Christmas my sister sent me a pink Afro wig, which I wore for special occasions, but mainly I was fine with my big brown head, and I rather missed it when my hair started to grow back after a change of drugs four months later.

The only bad experience was when a couple of ten-year-olds followed me up the street pointing, laughing and calling me 'Baldy'. But even that had a funny side. Watching Rob doing the honourable thing by running after them was bloody marvellous.

A footnote: I lost the hair on my head, my pubic hair, my eyebrows and lashes and my underarm hair. But do you think I could get rid of my leg hair? I still had to shave the buggers once a week.

What women want – attractive mastectomy bras

After nearly four months with only one breast, I arranged to meet Elizabeth, a consultant for the lingerie chain Lin & Barrett, who as well as selling super sexy bras to the average gal specialises in fitting women for breast prostheses.

I was very nervous at the prospect of buying a breast that hadn't previously been attached to a chicken. I mean, can you imagine? I had been shown a breast prosthesis at the hospital so I knew what to expect. They are flesh-coloured gel sacs shaped sort of like a breast. I was offered a range of styles and sizes, eventually opting for a D-cup teardrop to match my remaining left breast.

To achieve the most realistic effect the prosthesis is tucked into a pocket in the cup of a special mastectomy bra. If you've ever been to see the Cirque du Soleil in the Grand Chapiteau you'll be close to understanding the workings of the average mastectomy bra. Huge with wide, ugly straps, yards of hooks and eyes and big pockets to stop one's prosthesis causing a *faux pas* at parties by falling on to the floor, they are hardly built to flatter the ego or the body of the recently-operated-on cancer patient. They are so big they take two people to fold.

Here and now I want to start a campaign to get mastectomy bras made that women can feel feminine in. Having said that, although the bra and its cargo looked ugly without my clothes, once I put my jumper back on I looked fantastic. There really was no way of telling which was the real breast and which was the false one. This beat the pants off the aprons with big breasts attached that Rob and I had laughed about buying instead.

What women want – great friends and family

My wonderful mum had died of ovarian cancer three years before I was diagnosed. She was a very funny woman and a great friend. It is hard to imagine the fear and despair felt by my sister and my dad when they heard my news. How could this happen to us all again?

They were both on planes from their homes in England and New York within days of my surgery, and were strong and supportive throughout the whole ordeal, backing whatever decisions Rob and I made and never questioning the treatment we chose or the surgical options we went for later on. I love them madly.

It was during this time that I was able to sort the wheat from the chaff when it came to our friends. People did amazing things for us: delivering food parcels; gathering groups together for support; organising flight upgrades on a trip back to the UK; arranging a discount on an amazing beach house; arranging unlimited paid time off work during my chemo; ringing every day and sending flowers and cards. It is a wonderful feeling to know that you are loved by so many people, and I shall never forget it.

What women want – a cure for cancer

Enough said.

ELIZABETH BRODERICK

Elizabeth Broderick is a partner with the law firm Blake Dawson Waldron, where she has overall responsibility for the firm's online services and products. She has promoted work and life initiatives within the legal industry and in 2001 was appointed to the steering committee set up by the federal government to advise it on the OECD comparative study into family-friendly policies. In 2001 Elizabeth was Telstra's New South Wales Business Woman of the Year and winner of the Australian Telstra Corporate Sector Award for business women. She is married with two young children.

ELIZABETH BRODERICK

Life is in the Balance

Right from day one we were a close-knit family, three girls descended from a line of strong women. My twin sister, Jane, and I always argued over who was born first. Mum said Jane was and Dad said I was. It wasn't until Jane was applying for a passport that she saw her birth certificate and we finally knew. Beside Jane's name were the words 'first born'! I had always suspected this to be the case: she was the leader and the bossy one. It was for this very reason that my parents had decided to send us to separate schools. They thought it vital we develop as individuals.

From around the age of four, Jane and I and our younger sister, Carolyn, had been integrated into the family medical practice. My father was a nuclear medicine physician at a time when this specialty was just beginning. He established the nuclear medicine facility at St George Hospital while acting as superintendent. After a few years at St George Dad decided to launch out on his own. Necessity required all hands on deck. Mum, a physiotherapist, was drafted to act as the nuclear medicine technician, receptionist, office manager and bookkeeper, and we girls were enlisted to lick stamps, post mail, make drinks for patients and deliver reports to the hospital switchboard. Life was all go.

And so from a very early age we felt needed. We knew that part of the success of the surgery depended on us and on how well we carried out our tasks. We also understood from an early age the difference between playing at the back of the surgery and the professional behaviour required up front. I often wondered what it would be like to have parents who travelled to an office each day and performed a role which didn't involve me.

My experience of work and family during those early years formed the basis of my passion for combining the two. Another formative experience occurred during my last year at school. We had arranged a seminar at our school for other schoolchildren, extravagantly called 'University – Waste or Wonderland'. This was at a time when many seventeen-year-olds were questioning the value of further formal education and thinking instead of early-entry jobs that offered more money, such as in real estate, or more freedom of the spirit, like careers in the arts. We asked ten successful people, men and women from a wide range of occupations, to tell us about their journey and in particular the difficulties they had encountered. What an eye opener! For a school leaver with no direction but bursting with enthusiasm it was inspiring. They told stories of surprisingly tortuous journeys influenced by luck. While their stories were amazing, what I also noticed was that they all had something in common. They all had dreams of something bigger, they pursued those dreams, and they didn't let go, no matter how tough it got. It left me with two clear messages: aim high, and if you don't get it right the first time, keep on trying until you do.

When it came time to think seriously about the future, one of my main considerations was flexibility – I had to have a career that offered flexibility. I wanted the option to run my own business and integrate my family into it in the same way my parents had integrated me into theirs. How I came to the conclusion that the legal profession would offer me that is anyone's guess, but believe it I did and it was one of the main reasons I chose to become a lawyer. (Besides, physiotherapy was out as that was what my twin sister had chosen.) In truth, it would have been almost impossible to have selected a less family-friendly industry than law.

What I eventually decided upon was to combine a law degree with a computing science degree. I wasn't sure where this would take me but I dreamed technology would inexorably creep into law firms and I would be ready for the wave of opportunity it would create. Even so, most people thought I was mad. They said law would be the last thing to change. But as I learned from those memorable speakers at school, dreams are important and they can take you places.

In 1987, having worked in London for three years, I took a month's holiday in Australia. A month here was enough to convince me that I was missing out on a lifestyle I treasured, so I returned to Sydney in search of a job. I soon found one as a lawyer in the Research Department of Blake Dawson Waldron (BDW), a large, Australian-based law firm. The department had been newly created and hence was in a state of flux. This offered me the enormous opportunity to make of the job what I wanted.

In 1991, BDW appointed me head of a separate group known as the Legal Technology Group. It was envisaged that this group would be staffed by lawyers and computer professionals and would respond to the growing demand for new types of service – service that was underpinned by technology. We would develop a suite of online legal services aimed at major corporations.

The group initially comprised just my assistant and me, but at that time no other firms were taking any such initiative. We were on our way, pioneering new territory. It was exciting.

However, while the decision to pursue a non-mainstream area of legal practice brought rewards it wasn't all plain sailing. At the time I had started practising, being a lawyer in a non-mainstream area meant you were not offered partnership nor could you expect to be mentored to the same degree as a mainstream lawyer. Running a legal business requires all types of lawyers and I didn't think it was fair only one type should be rewarded. I wanted to be made a partner.

I pursued partnership for two years. The challenge was to convince the existing partners of the value of what I was doing. Certainly it wasn't mainstream, but I was still practising law. This required a degree of cultural change, for lawyers to think differently about the practice of law and to anticipate how delivering legal services might change in the future.

Part of me thought changing the culture was too hard and that I should go back to being a mainstream lawyer, where the career path and job function were well mapped out. But I returned to the wisdom I learned from those speakers at school – if at first you don't succeed, keep on trying.

I hung in there and I'm glad I did. After much agonising by the partnership and one false start, I was promoted to partner in July of 1995. I was the first legal technology lawyer from a non-mainstream area of practice to become a partner of a major law firm within Australia. A dream come true.

There is no doubt that the firm's decision to set up the Legal Technology Group was a wise one that has brought many benefits. Aside from generating significant revenue, the business has given Blake Dawson Waldron a point of differentiation from other big Australian law firms and an important competitive edge. Technology is now central to our positioning. However, I think our greatest advantage is that it has strengthened our relationship with our clients, who are also experiencing transformation of their organisations because of the impact of technology and the Internet.

But at one point it looked as if the Legal Technology Group was about to collapse. About five years after the group was established one of my lawyers dropped by to tell me she was pregnant. The same afternoon another senior manager gave me the same news. What they didn't know was that I was also pregnant. Three weeks later a fourth lawyer joined the queue.

I knew that if I couldn't accommodate them on some flexible basis during their maternity leave and return to work they would quit, either to become full-time parents or to join a less demanding and more family-friendly workplace. If that happened and we lost the valuable knowledge and expertise of all the key players, our Legal Technology Group would melt down. We had to get family-friendly and we had to do it quickly. I now had a perfect and solid business reason to construct a work environment that offered staff the flexibility they required and enabled some degree of integration of family life.

After the initial jokes about what was happening in the Legal Technology Group, both full-time and part-time staff sat down to begin developing a new way of working. We needed to ensure that, whatever we did, our business would continue in a profitable manner and there would be no diminution of service to our clients. It was also important to ensure that the full-time staff did not feel that they had to pick up the slack. There followed a period of uncertainty, of trialling different ways of working and of great flexibility on behalf of the firm and members of the group. We were desperate to make this work.

We brought two lawyers in from other offices to cover us over the maternity period. But we had to work out how our business could continue and meet the demands for flexibility that each person required. I knew exactly how my staff felt because I also felt that flexibility was the key to sustaining the business we had built.

We developed a system whereby the ultimate responsibility for matters rested with the individual, whether or not they worked full- or part-time. And, if a 'flexible worker' needed to come in on a non-designated work day, the arrangement was they could bring in the kids. They also agreed to carry a mobile phone when away from their home and to access their e-mail account at least once a day.

We established a telephone protocol where only calls of a certain nature were transferred to the flexible worker and other calls were dealt with elsewhere in the group. I wanted to ensure that each of our flexible workers maintained their previous position and level of seniority. I wanted them to remain just as committed to the firm as they had been previously.

We realised early on that we needed support staff who shared the vision for a new way of working and who could multi-skill. We had one wonderful junior secretary whose most relevant qualification was three years' nannying experience. She made sure the children loved coming into work by making it a great adventure. Now the children are at an age where they can be productive and carry out basic tasks and they do it with relish. Just as I had felt needed in the family business, our children feel needed in our legal business.

Even though these may seem like small steps, I have found that workplace flexibility builds a supportive and productive environment like nothing else. For me it has also bred a loyalty among my team that money could never buy. Nor have I lost an employee after maternity leave. They've all returned. I don't think I can emphasise enough the impact that this has had on the business.

And all this inside a major law firm!

It would be great to be able to say that we set out to make things better for women in law – to change the law firm culture of long hours, hard work, stress and often limited control. We didn't set out to do that but, surprisingly, that is in fact what is happening. People love the flexibility. They love combining family and work and no one is less productive as a result. There is simply no downside. At the beginning we were just trying to solve an immediate business problem – the problem of having half the legal team on maternity leave! Only when we solved the problem were we able to see that the patchwork of initiatives we had implemented had made an enormous difference and if applied elsewhere within the organisation would probably have the same effect.

Without such a wonderfully supportive human resources team the degree of organisational change would have been very limited. Although I acted as an agent for change, the initiatives would have stopped dead without their support. They believed that flexible work practices were the way of the future.

We now have seven part-time partners and approximately 10 per cent of all staff work part-time. The programs we have instigated have played their part in promoting and retaining employees, which has led to an annual saving in the cost of recruitment, selection and training conservatively estimated to be $1.7 million. During the past five years staff turnover has decreased from 28 per cent to 17 per cent. In particular, turnover of staff at the senior associate level, the level at which employees become most concerned about losing their life to work, significantly decreased to well below industry standards. As well, this year we won the Employer of Choice Award at the annual Law Awards.

I think the presence of more women in senior positions in business is bringing about a change in the way professional services firms and corporations are run. Most women recognise the importance of building community and a shared vision within the organisation. Many of the working and parenting initiatives that we established did just that. But it's not just about building community within the organisation. Extended communities which include clients and key suppliers and other market players are also integral to our success. To help make this happen, we set up a Working and

Parenting Group with the firm's support.

The Working and Parenting Group is open to all members of staff, their partners, clients and friends. The vision is to provide a forum for working parents to exchange ideas and to hear from leading experts on work and life issues. The forum also provides an opportunity to build relationships with our clients, who are also parents outside the confines of daily transactional business. We get to see each other in an entirely different light and to forge relationships on a different basis.

This year the group has hosted presentations by leading health professionals, including one by the head of the Metabolism and Obesity Clinic at Royal Prince Alfred Hospital on eating disorders in children and adolescents. We have also run three sessions by a forensic psychologist and ex-policeman on how dangerous men think. We have featured sessions by leading academics on balancing work and family demands such as child rearing, as well as the important issue of elder care. The part I love best about all these sessions is the question time. It is then that we start to develop a sense of community as the group tries to find solutions to each of the difficult parenting and caring situations we encounter. For the first time this year, the firm has allocated an expense budget for this group.

No business wants to lose talented staff, and when they leave they generally do so to pursue another job; to focus on parenting; or to pursue an alternative lifestyle. Traditionally, firms will try to retain valued staff who are thinking of leaving for other jobs with offers of more money or better positions. Yet the same drive to retain staff is not generally directed towards those who leave to take up parenting duties or to opt for lifestyle changes. Yet, with some foresight and flexibility, it is not hard for a business to accommodate the needs of these two groups and reap the benefits.

Surely the future viability of Australian business rests in part with our ability to introduce and offer widespread support for flexible workplace practices. There is a growing trend for people to question the wisdom of a life devoted to work. There has been a shift in thinking and these days people are more tuned in to the importance of achieving a balanced life. They are less prepared to kill themselves for the sake of career advancement.

For those approaching the end of their career the options have been limited. With the ageing of our population we can no longer let our most experienced and valuable people leave the work force completely. For these reasons I think flexibility in the workplace is perhaps the single most important issue facing Australian business. And looking at it globally, highly trained and skilled knowledge workers are in short supply. Why do workers posted overseas return to Australia or, alternatively, why do they stay in Australia? They don't come for the global deals. They come because this is where they want to live, where they want to bring up their children, where they want to integrate work and life. Australian business must support people in this decision. Not to do so is to ignore our unique point of difference in the global economy. Australia has a special lifestyle to offer, and without too much effort we could easily gain a reputation for offering the best work–life environment in the world.

I hope that in the next two to three years I won't need to argue the case for flexible working conditions, that it will be part of our mainstream culture.

But at the end of the day, it's not just about business.

It's about the future work–life environment we want for our children and our country. It's about parents and non-parents alike. It's about recognising the reason why people choose to live in Australia, about understanding our unique point of difference.

And it's about leaving the world a little bit better than we found it. Humans have a limited life span but significant social change lives on! Let's do our bit to make sure the next generation of Australians is not asked to choose between work and family.

SARAH O'HARE

Sarah O'Hare is an Australian supermodel who has walked the runways for most top designers and appeared in campaigns for famous names including Estée Lauder, Yves Saint Laurent, Ralph Lauren, L'Oréal and Wonderbra. In 1999 Sarah joined the prestigious Revlon family of spokes-models, and in 2001 she became ambassador for Bonds. Sarah made her film debut in 2001 in Universal's *Head Over Heels*. She maintains an active involvement in the Murdoch Children's Institute and is patron of the National Breast Cancer Foundation.

SARAH O'HARE

The Science of Saving Lives

Some of you may know me as Sarah O'Hare; others may know me as a spokeswoman and patron for the National Breast Cancer Foundation. But I also work with the Murdoch Children's Research Institute, and I'm going to talk about something that, while it may seem a little obscure, has tremendous implications for our future and the future of our children.

Imagine a child, a child who is dying of leukaemia. A bone marrow transplant could save her. But even if a donor can be found, she will still have to undergo immunotherapy, which basically means she must sleep in a sterile hospital room alone, without close contact with her parents or any other people.

Every day, children like this little girl, children with leukaemia and other serious illnesses, die waiting for donor organs. But there's another choice. Stem cells.

So what are stem cells? Stem cells are very special cells that can become any part of the human body. They can be used to produce new tissues or organs to replace damaged or diseased ones.

Most parts of the body cannot regenerate once they are diseased or damaged. And there are not enough donor organs for our sick children. But by using stem cells via cloning technology we can make new tissue genetically identical to the recipient's, so that the transplant is effectively the recipient's own tissue.

Cloning in this context means cloning tissue to save someone's life. It does not mean the cloning of whole human beings. So what's the problem? Why do some people think it's wrong to do that?

Stem cells come from the bunch of cells created after fertilisation and which will develop into an embryo. Each year in Australia, up to 1000 embryos left over from IVF procedures are destroyed. While researchers are studying other ways of obtaining stem cells, at the moment leftover IVF embryos are the most promising source of these miracle cells.

Many of us believe that embryo cells are special, as they symbolise a potential future human life. But while we should definitely proceed with caution, we Australians need to be sure we know the facts about stem cell research. Only then can we make informed choices about what it has to offer.

Stem cell research may ultimately save countless lives. Eventually, we could all stand to benefit: this research has the potential to develop treatments for adult conditions like heart disease, Alzheimer's, Parkinson's disease and stroke. It could give us the chance to produce new bone marrow, a new heart or a new liver, so that the long, painful and sometimes fruitless wait for a donor becomes a thing of the past.

Initially, I was wary of aligning myself with a cause. What difference could I really make? But I have met many children who would benefit from stem cell research, and they all stole my heart. Now I feel that, if I can use my profile to save one little kid's life, it's all been worthwhile.

For our children's future, we need to be informed about the groundbreaking research into stem cells. It's a science for saving lives.

This is an edited transcript of a speech Sarah gave at the *marie claire* What Women Want forum on 10 October 2001.

IMOGEN CLARK

Imogen Clark is a teacher and writer who lives in Canberra. She is married to an academic and has three grown children and one grandson. Imogen is the author of *Saving Jessie*, which was published by Random House in 1999 and is the story of her youngest daughter's battle with heroin.

Photograph: from the cover of *Saving Jessie*, courtesy Getty Images

IMOGEN CLARK

Someone's Daughter

I t's not every day that a mother decides to write a book about her daughter's life. Especially as the young woman in question, while talented, intelligent and attractive, was not a famous rock star or a sporting hero. At eighteen her achievements were few, her potential untapped. Instead, she was a heroin addict.

I had imagined someone else would have documented just what that meant for families, how to help, what to do, how to react and how to survive this truly devastating problem. But they hadn't. So, just as I had imagined that someone else's child would become the heroin addict, I became the someone else who wrote a book about it.

In March 1999 Random House published *Saving Jessie*. When I first asked my daughter Jess and then the rest of the family for permission to write the book I had no idea what it would mean for us to have our family life publicly scrutinised. Neither did they.

I realise now that our story is not so unusual. The community is coming to understand that just as alcoholism knows no social barriers, neither does heroin addiction. But in February 1996, I could not understand how our youngest of three children, loved and highly valued by her family, could be in this situation.

There had been signs that things were not going well. Her group of friends had changed, her performance at school had slackened, her appearance had become very alternative and she had begun associating with people from outside school who were older than she was. But many teenagers display similar behaviour, and it does not necessarily indicate drug use.

Our first indication that she was involved with drugs came when she was fifteen, after she went missing for a weekend. We had arranged to collect her at a certain time one Friday evening, but she had not shown up. An hour later she rang to tell me she was staying out that night and would return in the morning. We spent the night furious at what we saw as her rebelliousness, but never imagining it was more than that. Jessie didn't come home on Saturday either. It was Sunday evening before our family tracked her down and the police returned her. We learned much later that she had taken an acid trip and was still too disoriented to return home on Saturday.

Jessie had been with a 34-year-old drug dealer known to the police, who had befriended her at the skate park next to her school. The police informed us that she had been smoking cannabis on a daily basis and needed to go into a detoxification centre. Feeling they must know best and certainly knowing no better, we reluctantly agreed. My daughter agreed too, but it is true to say she would have agreed to anything, so keen was she to make amends for her wayward weekend.

Jessie was placed in a detox centre with middle-aged male alcoholics, a move that now even the police would say was inappropriate. She left, at her instigation and with our support, after only five days.

At no time did the police or Jessie's school counsellor, in whom I'd confided, suggest that she seek any other kind of assistance. Naively I thought the few days in the detox centre and Jessie's extreme remorse for our concern and worry was all that was needed for her 'to pull herself together'.

For the next three years Jessie's life had a semblance of normalcy. She attended school, was involved in theatre and music and worked in the local supermarket on Sundays. We felt she was probably still experimenting with drugs, but always assumed (and wanted to assume) that it was cannabis, which we had assured ourselves was a relatively harmless pursuit.

However, when Jessie was seventeen she told us she needed to return to a detox centre. She assured us that it was not for heroin but for her experimentation with a variety of drugs. That same year she dropped out of school and temporarily, against our wishes, left home.

Jessie didn't wish to alarm us so she was always careful to shelter us from what she was doing and she covered her tracks well. At one stage she moved briefly to Melbourne. Only later we discovered that she had been terrified by the number of heroin-related deaths in the city where we live and thought that moving might solve her problem with drugs.

One evening in February 1996, when Jessie was flat-sitting for an acquaintance, she failed to show up for an arranged dinner. She had cancelled the night before, and as Jessie was usually quite reliable we became concerned. I drove over to her flat, waited for her to return and confronted her. It was then that she told me the shattering news that she was addicted to heroin.

We were so much more fortunate than most parents, because Jessie realised her life was in complete disarray and she wanted to stop using. We did not have to deal with a child who was not yet ready to face up to her addiction. But we had no idea how to help her. The problem seemed overwhelming.

Initially we felt it was not appropriate to discuss what was happening in our lives with others, except with a few of our most trusted friends. Our child was doing something that was illegal and widely condemned, and even though friends were kind and caring (and if they were judgmental they kept their judgments to themselves), they had no notion of the agony that parents of addicts live with. It is not only the risk of sudden overdose that is so distressing, but the disordered, dysfunctional lifestyle that inevitably accompanies addiction to illegal substances. Had our daughter had any other illness which endangered her life there would have been widespread understanding and support. But Jessie's illness was heroin addiction, and we weren't confident we would receive the same level of understanding.

So we sought advice and emotional support from drug counsellors. They helped us realise that it was our daughter's choice to use drugs and that it was up to her to change her behaviour. We couldn't do it for her. Nevertheless, while we could rationalise that it was Jessie's choice, we felt an overwhelming sense of failure and guilt. It seemed there were few more public indicators of parental failure than a child's heroin addiction.

The counsellors advised us not to give Jessie money and gently prepared us for the likelihood that she would continue to use. But at no time did anyone tell us what was advisable for her to do in order to recover or what we could do to help her.

Over the next three years we watched, cared, supported and suffered as Jessie did. We made mistakes and bumbled along as best we could as she struggled to become and remain clean.

Initially we thought the solution was simply for me to take Jessie away to a friend's isolated farm to look after her as she detoxed. We assumed that she would detox and then just resume a normal life. We knew no more than the average person in the community who has never been confronted with this problem. We certainly didn't realise that addiction was a chronic, relapsing condition. Gradually we came to understand.

Jessie went to live interstate with her older brother, to try and break the ties with her using friends. Then she tried several rehabilitation centres, but was repeatedly asked to leave after breaking the rules. At one stage she worked and stayed clean for nine months before relapsing once again. Finally, in January 1998, Jessie completed a three-month program at a women-only rehabilitation centre in Sydney. She then moved into nearby supported housing run by the Salvation Army, and lived on her own in a clean bedsit with everything supplied that a recovering addict who has nothing may need.

With help from the support worker, to whom she had daily access, she had to learn what others take for granted: how to shop on a tight budget, how to pay bills on time, how to live responsibly. Jessie tells me now how hard it was, with all her emotional energy directed towards staying clean. Sometimes she attended two Narcotics Anonymous (NA) meetings a day, as she resolved on waking to not use 'just for today'. Sometimes, she tells me, her resolution was simply to not use 'just for the next hour'.

Jessie became heavily involved in NA, soon becoming convenor of a women's meeting and attending interstate conventions. She had a wonderful sponsor, a woman with two young children who was eight years clean. They had constant telephone contact, on one occasion the sponsor appearing on Jessie's doorstep within minutes when she judged a phone call had not been sufficient. For many months Jessie had dinner at her sponsor's place on alternate Sundays. Later, Jessie assumed this role for another young woman in NA.

Jessie described her first year clean as both the worst and best year of her life. She also had some luck. Having decided to move out of supported housing after fifteen months, Jessie, with some friends, found a house to rent. As they were signing the contract, the real estate agent saw Jessie's NA one-year-clean tag on her key ring. Jessie was sure it would mean forfeiting the house, so she was touched when he handed it back to her, saying quietly, 'Eight years clean. AA.' They got the house.

After some time, as Jessie grew stronger, she began an acting course, which went a long way to restoring her confidence and self-esteem while giving her a sense of purpose. The royalties from *Saving Jessie* funded it, which seemed appropriate to us.

Jessie has now been clean for more than four years. On her clean birthday we send her flowers – big, extravagant flowers with a lavish message which always makes her cry as she reads it and me cry as I write it – acknowledging her commitment and effort and how proud we are of her for turning her life around. She's not perfect, but our family are all members of her fan club. Whatever else Jessie may achieve in her life, very little will be more important than staying clean.

Recently, Jessie decided that she no longer wanted to be a member of NA, which has been such an important part of her life for the last few years. She no longer wants to be defined as a recovering addict and wants to resume a lifestyle like any other young woman, no longer going to meetings twice a week, no longer avoiding alcohol. She feels her using days belong to another time in her life and she wants to move on.

Only time will tell if she is right to do without the support that has been so vital to her. I have met with parents and talked to many groups at meetings and conferences, but one parent stands out. Her son had been clean for eight years when his relationship broke up and within months he was in jail for armed robbery. Can any parent say it is really over?

By far the hardest part of writing *Saving Jessie* was presenting Jessie with the manuscript to read. We took it to her in Sydney, Jessie having decided that it was better for her to read it where she had a strong support base. She was then only eight months clean. We had dinner and dropped her home, armed with the manuscript and pencils and Post-its for marking sections she wanted to discuss. From the outset Jess and I had an agreement that this was my perception of what had happened and she did not have to correct my misconceptions unless she wanted to.

At one o'clock the next afternoon she rang me, having read through the night. There were Post-its everywhere, but she wanted only one phrase removed to protect her boyfriend. I felt relief. I think she probably felt shocked that this was actually going to be published. I now realise how vulnerable she was then and how ill-equipped she was to make a decision and be assertive. Her support worker also read the manuscript as Jessie's nominated advocate.

But Jessie never wavered from her first reaction that if the book could help people deal with what we were dealing with she wanted it written. She still stands by that decision now, but it has not always been easy for her. She finds it uncomfortable that acquaintances feel much closer to her than she does to them. We have all found that imbalance of information awkward.

Jess rarely discloses that a book has been written about her and then only to those she feels she has known long enough and can trust. Recently she began a new relationship, one she feels will be very important. Very early on and unavoidably she let it slip to him. The next evening he returned, red-eyed with flowers and chocolates, overwhelmed by what he had read, having bought the book immediately. Later Jessie rang me, dismayed at such early, unintentional disclosure, but buoyed by his caring, supportive response.

Jessie has not always felt positive about it. Some time ago, when she could bring herself to read it again, she felt great anger that details of her life were there for others to read. That part of her life has been encapsulated forever, but it is no longer her reality. Generally, though, she tells me that she sees it as my book and she separates herself from it.

My husband has also found it difficult at times. Never once

wavering in his support, and offering constant reassurance after the book was published when I was having misgivings about such exposure, he still found the invasion of his privacy uncomfortable, especially among colleagues who knew about the book and its subject matter but chose not to acknowledge it to him. What I had written became the accepted story of our family, a story in which he had had no voice. While he had read and approved the manuscript, he had found it so heart-rending he had not been able to suggest changes or even indicate that his perception of events was different in any way.

Mismatches in perception became very clear some months after publication, when Jessie was interviewed for a story in a Sunday paper as an example of someone who had overcome adversity. In essence, the story that appeared was the story I had written, but the detail was different and disturbing. The reality of Jessie's using lifestyle was so much worse than she had told us. After reading the interview we felt the need to touch base with her immediately, and within days we had travelled to Sydney to see her.

I always had modest ambitions for my book. I wanted someone to take it seriously enough to review it. Instead, it was reviewed many times, nominated for six writing awards, short-listed for one and sold overseas. An extract was published in the *Daily Telegraph*, and Reader's Digest chose it as one of their condensed non-fiction titles. It is on the year ten reading list in at least one state school and is used in many other high schools. It is used widely by professionals in counselling their clients and their parents. I have had letters from police officers and ambulance officers who say they now can deal with addicts with some understanding. And I've received many thanks from parents who have gained some strength from reading about us.

I have no magic answer to drug addiction and I feel wary of anyone who claims one. What I have learnt is that one approach does not suit all and, unfortunately, nothing will suit some. It is very sobering to realise that it is only the most resilient – a small percentage of addicts – who recover to lead fully functioning lives. Others, if they do recover, do so to lesser or greater degrees.

Governments need to be innovative rather than conservative in legislation. Our community needs safe injecting rooms to minimise the risk of overdose, to keep our addicts alive, to put them in touch with agencies which can help them if they choose to seek help. We need a controlled heroin trial, to see if it is a viable alternative for hard-core, long-term addicts for whom nothing else has worked. Abstinence will never be achievable for some. We also need funding for more rehabilitation programs, so that addicts and their families are not faced with the agony of an interminable wait once the decision has been made to seek help. Critically, we need government-funded, supported housing for recovering addicts, once they have left rehabilitation centres, when the job of rebuilding a clean life is only just beginning.

And our community needs to exercise some compassion. Our addicts are all someone's son or daughter who, for a variety of reasons, has lost their way. It is only with compassion that they may find it again.

LIBBI GORR

Libbi Gorr is best known for her work as radio and television adventurer Elle McFeast. As producer, writer, singer and performer, Libbi is well known to both Australian and international audiences for her interviews and satirical observations on life and society. Her television credits included 'Live & Sweaty', 'McFeast' and 'McFeast Live'. She has co-produced and starred in numerous documentaries, including 'Portrait of a Power Pussy' and 'Alive & Kicking'. In 2001 she created two specials, 'The Queen and I' and 'Sex Cells'. Libbi has performed in sell-out seasons of *The Vagina Monologues* in Sydney, Melbourne and Adelaide.

LIBBI GORR

Be Cheeky

Since the voice of Australian women was first heard in 1894 (the year women were first given the vote in South Australia), it's grown and it's developed as we have as a nation. It's refined itself and it's become more uniform in its quest for answers. So much so that I reckon that if you pressed an ear to the collective hopes and dreams of us as Australian women, you would hear one very loud refrain echoing across the land. One loud chorus expressing our deepest concern, reflecting the issue that troubles us most. Asking the question that we need to know the answer to before we can securely go out and face the world. I think you know the one that I'm talking about. 'Does my bum look big in this?'

Yeah, yeah, I'm writing about body image. Yep, I got the deep topic. And as you can see I'm amply qualified to do so. This is because I actually – you might find this difficult to believe – but I actually have a shocking image. It's appalling. Every morning I wake up, I look in the mirror and I see Pamela Anderson. You know, it's just not up to scratch. And the reason is because my body defies the law that we as women have been indoctrinated with since we were very, very small. That rule that's meant to determine our success in life, that's meant to give us the blueprint for getting what we want as women. The rule that can be condensed into six tiny little words. They're scary so hold on to your seat: 'You no skinny, you no winny.'

Now, I don't know whether you've noticed but I've got a little bit of a design flaw. Oh, laugh all you want, but I actually have a big bottom. No, I tell a lie, it's a *very* big bottom. And you may laugh all you like, Sarah O'Hare, but you have no idea what it's like to have a big bottom. It's like being stalked. It's always behind you.

This aberration, this affliction that I've been blessed with is actually the result of something that I've never spoken about in public before. I actually have a fairly common eating disorder. I am what you would call a gutless bulimic, in that I couldn't throw up even if I wanted to.

My bottom is actually indicative of a greater issue that affects us all. It's the issue of body image and self-esteem, and it brings me to my point, which is the war that women wage upon themselves, the dreadful one of body image and self-esteem. It can affect everything a woman does.

And we don't just do it to ourselves. We terrorise other women with this sort of stuff. Like the girl that you meet who you haven't seen since you've been at school together and you go, 'Hi, oh, how great to see you,' kiss, kiss. And she looks you up and down, smiles really sweetly, flashes her engagement ring and says, 'My, aren't you looking healthy.' She might as well just look you square in the eye and say, 'My God, haven't you porked up, you fat pig.'

For this I blame the Duchess of Windsor, because it was she who said that a woman can never be too skinny, too rich or too blonde. But if we had the opportunity to ask the female icons of our era – of glamour, Princess Diana; of sexiness, Marilyn Monroe; of attitude and sass, Paula Yates – they would probably say that you can never be too comfortable in your own skin, you can never be too valued for what you can contribute, and you can never be too loved for who you are on the inside.

The thing that's scorched into my mind and into my soul from the September 11 terrorist attacks is how the people in the aeroplanes rang those they loved. Because that's what's important. They wanted to know that they were loved and they wanted to tell their loved ones the same, and it was that security, that comfort, that saw them through to their horrible ends.

So I want to feel secure that we, as women, are going to use our collective voice not to terrorise our inner souls when we go and try on a pair of bathers and suddenly lose them in the process. I want to know that we're going to use our voice to do something productive for ourselves and for each other. You know, to give ourselves security in the things that we value the most in terms of our liberty, in terms of our lifestyle and in terms of the people that we love. And that is the power that only comes from within. And I'm not talking about securing that just for Australian women, I'm talking about securing that for women across the road, across the world. Let's face it, we are a global brand.

So I'd like you to take a stand, if you would – in fact, I'm going to take this one. And I'm going to ask you all now to take off your clothes, in your own time. I want you to take off your clothes and I want you to stand in front of that full-length mirror and I want you to shake it all about. Just shake it all about and then I want you to walk slowly towards that full-length mirror like this, and then I want you to turn, and I want you to remember two things. Not one – two. I want you to remember that your self-worth cannot be measured in kilograms, and I want you to remember that when Cupid shoots his arrow, he's aiming for your heart, not your hips. Because when you recognise your personal power, and when you have that confidence, when you have that security, you know you may not be skinny and you may not be rich, but with a little bit of lemon juice and a good hairdresser you can all have a go at being blonde.

This is an edited transcript of a speech Libbi gave at the *marie claire* What Women Want forum on 10 October 2001.

JESSICA ROWE

Jessica Rowe is a news presenter for Network Ten. Jessica has always been passionate about news and current affairs and has a degree in communications from Bathurst's Charles Sturt University. Currently she's completing a Masters degree in International Studies at the University of Sydney. Jessica loves her family, reading, high heels and her cat, Audrey.

JESSICA ROWE

*There's Light in the
Darkness of Mental Illness*

Mental illness. Something that's extremely close to my heart and an issue that affects a lot of women. Mental illness has an enormous impact on families, particularly children, whose stories often remain forgotten and unheard.

Mental illness is isolating. It leaves people feeling powerless and alone. That's why I'm here tonight, to tell you my story about how mental illness impacted upon my childhood. How it left me feeling helpless and out of control, but how at the same time it gave me strength and courage.

It's not a glamorous topic – there's nothing beautiful about someone suffering a mental illness, and psychiatric hospitals aren't very inspiring places. But one of the most beautiful and inspiring people I know has a mental illness and that person is my mother. Mum sees her illness as just a part of her life.

It doesn't define her life. There's no cure, but she makes every day count.

I realised that Mum wasn't like other mothers when I was aged about eight or nine. My bedroom was right next to hers and every night I lay in bed listening to her sobbing herself to sleep. I would creep out, put my head next to her door and listen to her cry. I wasn't sure what to do. Eventually I would make my way back to bed and curl myself into a tight bundle, but I'd find it impossible to go to sleep until I knew that Mum had stopped crying.

Mum has bipolar disorder. It used to be known as manic depression. Fortunately, it's an episodic illness with periods of remission. So there are times when Mum's well. It's a condition that gives her periods of frantic manic energy. There'd be times when she'd stay up all night cleaning the flat, wearing next to nothing. Another time she became fixated on the idea of making hair clips for my two sisters and me. Not just one or two, but twenty or thirty different designs.

But these periods of high manic energy were very brief. Mum would come crashing down into a deep, dark depression. Her face would look drawn, her eyes would be sunken with big black rings underneath. She then existed on no sleep. Her appetite would start to go. She'd lose her sense of smell. Any food in her mouth would make her gag. Any sound around her became amplified. Talking, traffic, music became unbearably loud for her. Gradually she'd just withdraw and find it harder to interact with people around her.

I was ten when Mum had her first breakdown. My sisters were aged nine and six. Because Mum went to hospital, we went to stay with my father and my stepmother. At the time it just seemed like an extended sleep-over at their place, and part of the adventure included picking up my sisters from school to visit Mum in the hospital. We'd have to take a bus and a train, and I remember being frightened because I had to ring the bell on the bus, and I had to stand on top of my suitcase to reach it. But being the eldest I knew I had to.

From then on, when everyday living became too hard for her, Mum would end up in the psychiatric hospital, sometimes for three months at a time. The trips to the hospital to visit her were very hard. Being the eldest, I felt I had to put on a brave face for my mum and for my two younger sisters. So early on, as shy as I was, I assumed the job of being the strong, brave one in the family. It was a role that put enormous pressure on me. My heart used to sink when we'd walk down the hospital corridor approaching Mum's door. I'd be hoping, wondering, praying. What state would I find her in? Would she be silent and sad? Would she just sob or would she also try to be brave? The toughest part for me was seeing her in such a state of despair and feeling powerless to do anything about it.

When Mum was very ill, it just wasn't safe for her to be at home. There were times when Mum was unwell but still at home, and as I got older I'd notice the warning signs, so I'd do more to help, like organise the cooking and the shopping. Because this crept up on me over time, the added responsibility really didn't seem that unusual. As well, we had beautiful family and friends who'd come by, drop off food, perhaps stay the night.

When I was about twelve I came home from school one day to find Mum upset because she hadn't been able to cross the road on her own. She had become really frightened of the traffic. She had been stuck in the middle of the road, unable to take one step forward or back. I was determined for her to know that she could do it, so I took her hand, walked back down the hill with her and helped her cross the road.

As a teenager, I felt even more devastated by Mum's illness. I was never embarrassed by it, though. I realised that her depression came in a cycle that would often see her unwell once a year and in hospital. There was a time when I was studying for my Higher School Certificate and Mum was going downhill very fast. The doctors were trying different medications but nothing was working. I came home from school and I'd forgotten my keys, so I called out for Mum to let me in. She couldn't walk to the front door. She crawled halfway there, becoming more and more upset. She managed to find the keys then threw them at me down the stairs, abusing me.

I couldn't believe it. I was so upset. My simple request to be let into the house had made her worse. It was terrifying to have the woman who I placed on a pedestal, the woman I thought was meant to look after *me*, disintegrate before my eyes, unable to cope with the simplest of tasks.

A terrible revelation was when Mum told me that she'd thought about suicide on many occasions. But the thought of us, her daughters, stopped her. It gives me some relief to know that, as a family, we gave her a reason to keep living.

The sense of helplessness and powerlessness I feel about Mum's illness hasn't changed, even though I'm older and hopefully a little wiser. I still get anxious when I notice the warning signs. I still feel despair and anger. A sense of it not being fair. Why did it have to happen to my mum, to me, to my family?

It wasn't easy as a child coping with Mum's illness. It forced me to grow up very, very quickly and I lost a big part of my childhood. But I found support and I've seen counsellors to help me deal with those issues.

So what do I want? Discussion. It's vital for people to realise they're not alone. The more people feel they can openly talk about mental illness, the faster the myths and the stigma about it will disappear.

And I want support, for all those touched by mental illness, both the sufferers and their families. It's essential for people to know that help is there. Because it's possible to use the strength and courage we find within ourselves to not only survive but to thrive and lead a positive and enriching life.

So it's my hope, my wish, my dream that everyone who has a loved one with mental illness receives the help and support they need to find some light in the darkness. Just as I have.

This is an edited transcript of a speech Jessica gave at the *marie claire* What Women Want forum on 10 October 2001.

PRU GOWARD

A national affairs journalist and political commentator and broadcaster for nineteen years, Pru Goward is currently the Federal Sex Discrimination Commissioner. Pru has worked closely on issues of women's rights, heading the federal women's policy advisory unit of the Office of the Status of Women from 1997 to 1999. During the past ten years Pru has run her own media management company and has been a part-time lecturer in Broadcast Journalism at the University of Canberra. She is married with three children.

Pru Goward

Juggling Act

I had my first two children at such an unlikely young age we grew up together. But inevitably when I went to work the mother juggle kicked in. I was forced to develop a preference for early morning shifts in order to be with my daughters after school. On many occasions when I was working for the ABC I would conduct an interview with a federal minister on air, rush home at 8.30 am to take the girls to school, tear back to Parliament House, prepare for the midday program, then rush to collect the children after school for music lessons. Afternoon shifts allowed me to do tuckshop duty, and on those days my daughters would come to Parliament House after school, get treated to visits to the (then) prime minister's office and pretend to do their homework in the corner of the studios. Music lessons required that the coverage of a national crisis be squeezed in around delivery and collection times. Thank goodness it was Canberra.

It was complicated and often difficult but I managed. So do millions of other women, who, despite an array of complexities, barriers and frustrations, manage to both do paid work and raise children. In fact, in Australia a majority of women with dependants work: overall 35.4 per cent of mothers work at least part-time when their children are aged less than twelve months (unpublished Australian Bureau of Statistics (ABS) data, 1996). By the time children are four years old, 48 per cent of their mothers are in the paid work force or seeking employment, a figure that jumps to 71 per cent of partnered women once their children begin primary school (ABS, 1996).

We're not bad at looking after the interests of women who want to remain at home and raise their children. And we're getting better at ensuring women in careers are able to compete on an equal footing. But meeting the needs of the majority of women – those who choose to combine parenting with work – has proven to be more of a challenge, and much remains to be done. Every working mother reading this will know exactly what I mean.

The right of Australian women to make such a choice is guaranteed in theory by the law and underpinned by universal suffrage and our country's robust democracy. Our right to exercise choice and suffer no discrimination is protected by the *Sex Discrimination Act* 1984. That is the Act I am responsible for promoting, protecting and applying as Sex Discrimination Commissioner.

Under the Act, sex discrimination is when someone is treated less favourably because of their sex, marital status, pregnancy or their potential to become pregnant. Two forms of discrimination are identified: direct and indirect. Both are illegal.

Direct discrimination would include, for example, discrimination that bars a woman from working, such as the bar that prevented married women from working in the public service (a bar that wasn't lifted until the late 1960s).

It is increasingly rare for institutions to directly exclude women or to permit them fewer or inferior rights. But there are exceptions: sporting associations (such as golf clubs), certain social clubs, religious institutions and, in some cases, state laws (such as the law that prevents women boxing in NSW). These voluntary organisations and jurisdictions are exactly those that are exempted from the reach of the *Sex Discrimination Act*. This suggests to me that there remains a view in society that men and women can and should be treated differently, and that when that view can be given effect, it is. The indignity of women golfers only being allowed on the greens for certain periods may appear trivial but serves to bear out the small-mindedness of discrimination. We may joke about it but the exclusion of women from voluntary clubs, institutions and religious bodies is a reminder that direct discrimination continues.

At least direct discrimination is easy to recognise. *Indirect* discrimination is more insidious, making it far more difficult to deal with. It often exists in the form of reduced choice, and it operates in particular against mothers who work in paid employment. Such indirect barriers may not have been created to stop women participating in work or to make their participation more difficult, but they may have that effect. Indirect discrimination against mothers in the workplace may include things like:

- insufficient or no financial support during maternity

- no guarantee of a job when a woman returns to paid work after maternity leave
- difficulty accessing affordable childcare
- unsuitable work hours
- inflexible work conditions that prevent mothers from taking time off for family reasons
- no facilities for working mothers to breastfeed or express milk.

There are still many employers who believe that women do not work as productively during pregnancy and either demote or dismiss them, or deny them training or otherwise allow their careers to stagnate. It comes as something of a shock to many independent and confident young women when, on entering parenthood, they discover a whole new world of discrimination or barriers to work. Indirect discrimination against working mothers is invidious, especially given that reproduction benefits society as a whole. Motherhood is not a motherhood statement for nothing.

There are limits to the law's capacity to prevent indirect discrimination. For example, under the *Sex Discrimination Act* it is illegal to discriminate against a person on the basis of their family responsibilities by dismissing them from employment. However, it is not illegal for a business to fail to provide conditions that enable women to both work and meet their family responsibilities. Dismissing someone because of their family responsibilities is a form of discrimination that is reasonably easy to deal with because it is a clear breach of the Act. But because the *Sex Discrimination Act* does not set out in detail laws against discrimination based on family responsibilities it is difficult to protect people when it happens in a way that is not so obvious.

Discrimination on the basis of family responsibilities often goes hand in hand with indirect sex or pregnancy discrimination. And a significant proportion of indirect pregnancy and sex discrimination complaints received by the Human Rights and Equal Opportunity Commission (HREOC) relate to women's family responsibilities. But because failing to provide family-friendly working conditions is not against the law, the HREOC cannot take any action beyond trying to encourage employers to do the right thing, via education and public discussion.

So what would a family-friendly workplace look like? For a start it might provide affordable childcare, paid maternity leave for a reasonable length of time and flexible working hours and conditions. At the moment Australian employers are not required to provide affordable childcare facilities. Likewise, private sector employers are not required to provide paid maternity leave, although they are obliged to provide twelve months' unpaid leave to all permanent female staff who have been employed for more than a year so they can look after new-born children. Flexible work hours and conditions remain the exception rather than the rule. However, businesses are slowly starting to see the benefits of family-friendly work practices for some employees. That is because they realise it is good for their business. It costs less to recruit and keep high calibre people than to continually hire and train newcomers. It's an argument that most employers can relate to so it is a mystery why there are still businesses who continue to ignore the benefits family-friendly practices can bring.

The next most obvious question is what is the government doing about it. Australia is a signatory to the United Nations Convention on the Elimination of All Forms of Discrimination Against Women but has entered a reservation in regard to paid maternity leave. This means Australia has agreed to abide by the conditions of the convention with the exception that it will not pass laws in favour of paid maternity leave. Incidentally, Australia has a second reservation concerning the involvement of women in armed combat.

In regard to childcare, the federal government spends well over $1 billion annually in subsidies, while some state governments provide additional childcare subsidies. Most of this money goes to part-time workers seeking part-time childcare hours.

As well, the federal government provides some financial assistance to women on the birth of each child and at eighteen months following initial childhood vaccinations. There are also tax rebates available to some families and additional tax rebates for single-income families. Recently the government announced further tax relief for women having their first child, which adds to the financial support available to women, although it may not qualify as paid maternity leave.

But while there is government assistance for both mothers who work and mothers who stay at home, women who do their sums will find there is more assistance for those who do not do paid work. Currently government assistance – mostly in the form of childcare subsidies – for families in which mothers do paid work averages about two-thirds of the assistance, mainly through tax relief, available to families in which the mother does not do paid work. Understandably, some of this gap reflects the lower family incomes of many single-income families. But for a family on an income of, say, \$80 000, the government assistance enjoyed by the single-breadwinner family is greater than the assistance enjoyed by a family on the same income, but with two income earners.

The question for all Australians is whether our current laws and the government support families receive protect working mothers from indirect discrimination. It's part of a wider question about what we want to achieve by reducing the obstacles for working women.

To answer this question we need to take into account the interests of women themselves, knowing they will make a variety of choices, as well as the interests of employers, taxpayers and society over the long and short term. Then we must balance these various interests against the competing demands on limited government resources. Together these various interests make up the national interest.

Protecting the national interest is the task we entrust to our government, and it involves balancing the rights and interests of one group, such as women, against the rights and interests of others. Of course, the rights and interests of women are vitally important to the national interest. Females constitute more than 50 per cent of the population and just under 50 per cent of the total work force, so the weight of their interests should be formidable. The interests of working mothers in particular are one and the same as the national interest in the following ways:

- **Addressing declining population growth** – Australia's fertility rate is currently about 1.75 children per woman, down from a peak of 3.6 in 1961. The replacement fertility rate is around 2.1. Some people believe that women are having fewer babies as a result of the financial, professional or social disadvantages families experience. Another view is that our declining birth rate is a consequence of general uncertainty in the job market. Still others argue that providing paid maternity leave would encourage women to have more children, especially those women who are unwilling to have one or more children due to a loss of income.

- **Health and social welfare** – A large number of women are now in the paid work force during their pregnancy and many return, at least part-time, within twelve months of giving birth. It is in the interests of both mother and child that women be able to take a decent break before and after childbirth.

- **Human resource management** – It has been proven that paid maternity leave can reduce staff losses and encourage women to return to the work force earlier. Human rights in this case make good business sense. With increasing numbers of women graduates (50 per cent in many cases) employers can no longer expect to have a top quality work force if they ignore the requirements of half their potential recruits.

- **Investment in education** – We all invest heavily in education, especially higher education. For women to lose a significant period of earning time and then possibly never reach their full potential earnings is to reduce the return on that investment.

- **Fairness for all employees** – About 30 per cent of Australian women receive employer-funded paid maternity leave, mainly in the public sector and larger private organisations. While this is an improvement on past figures, paid maternity leave is still not common in those industries that employ mainly women, such as retail, accommodation and hospitality. This causes inequality between women.

- **Addressing systemic discrimination** – Women continue to bear the major responsibility for the care of children. So even though men and women share family responsibilities, the economic impact of parental leave tends to fall disproportionately on women.

If we want to meet our country's greater social and national interests we need to do more than provide sixteen weeks' paid leave. We also need unpaid periods of maternity leave, financial assistance with childcare and legal provisions for breastfeeding or the expressing of breast milk in the workplace. We need to ensure that part-time workers have access to training and promotional opportunities, and have industrial trade-offs that give carer–workers greater flexibility with their hours. Perhaps we need to see some superannuation trade-offs between working spouses, to ensure that the primary parent's long-term financial independence is not more limited than that of the primary income earner's. As well, perhaps there needs to be some other provision for income security at retirement age for people who have taken time out of paid work to raise children.

Some people have argued that women choose lower paid positions for the non-financial trade-offs like flexibility to allow for family responsibilities. And yes, it is true that many women raising a family are happy working less than full-time (Ilene Wolcott & Helen Glezer, *Work and Family Life: Achieving Integration*, Australian Institute of Family Studies,

Melbourne, 1995). However, this often means they are penalised for the remainder of their working life.

Surely none of us would accept that those women who bear the greater responsibility for raising Australia's families should be penalised in this way. And by penalised I mean not making enough to make a decent contribution to superannuation, spending the rest of their time in the work force struggling to catch up, or unable to take advantage of training or promotional opportunities because employers no longer take their ambitions seriously.

With obstacles like these, it's no wonder that so many women are putting off having children. They know they will immediately be relegated to the bottom of the working class, from where they may never return.

It's not just women who are now demanding that paid work become more family-friendly; it is also their partners and families. It is often said that Australian society is increasingly besieged by the pressures and strains of modern life. Providing a secure and happy environment for the upbringing of children is a large part of that pressure and strain. So is the pressure on women trying to meet a score of conflicting aims.

It's time we embraced the needs of modern Australian families, whatever choices they make between paid work and child rearing. Meeting the aspirations and needs of working mothers is a huge part of that challenge. Enhancing choices for women must mean that their families and society will also be better off.

Choice, so fundamental to our way of life, will then have real meaning for all Australians.

Natasha Stott Despoja

Born in Adelaide, Natasha Stott Despoja received her political grounding at Adelaide University. In 1995 at the age of twenty-six she became the youngest woman to enter federal parliament, having been elected to represent the Australian Democrats in the Senate. She was elected deputy leader of the Democrats in 1997 then leader in 2001. In 2001 she was the only Australian to be named in the Top 100 Global Leaders of Tomorrow by the World Economic Forum.

NATASHA STOTT
DESPOJA

Women Still on the Verge . . .

I congratulate *marie claire* for the work the magazine has done to promote equality between men and women in the workforce in Australia. Magazine articles like 'Inequality at Work' and 'Punished for Being Pregnant', stories no Australian woman can afford to miss, help inform us, but they also put pressure on governments and businesses to provide family-friendly work environments.

But when I opened last month's magazine and saw the title 'The World's Wackiest Politicians', I was a little nervous. Thank you for not including me! The fact is, in this day and age, being female and being a Member of Parliament still seems wacky to some. We are still a novelty. We are more likely to be asked about our personal lives or our marital status than are our male colleagues, or have our clothing discussed by the media. We are still asked questions like: 'Well, what

happens if you have children and you want to be a Member
of Parliament?' (I like one politician's response, which was:
'Well, I'd put them in a cupboard all day. What do you
think?') But my personal favourite is: 'Did you go into politics
to meet a husband?' Now, despite the calibre available, I did
not.

There are lots of reasons why women do not go into my
profession, and more often than not it is because the work
environment is not family-friendly. Look at Parliament
House. We have a meditation room, a dry cleaner, a hairdresser and a gym, but no childcare facilities.

Unfortunately, women are still under-represented, not just
in politics but in all decision-making bodies, in particular in
business and industry. Only 10 per cent of Australia's board
members are women (Korn/Ferry survey, 2001), and only 1.3
per cent of top executive positions in Australian companies
are held by women (United Nations report on women in
management, *Breaking Through the Glass Ceiling*, reported
in *The Age*, 14 August 2001, page 4).

We still have a highly segregated workforce and women
tend to be concentrated in the low-skilled, low-paid and
casual positions. Our work and management practices remain
some of the most family-*unfriendly* in the entire world.
Women in full-time jobs still earn around 20 per cent less
than men for doing the same work, and this has not changed
during the past six years or so.

A Human Rights and Equal Opportunity Commission
report entitled *Pregnant and Productive: It's a Right Not a Privilege to Work While Pregnant* looked into the issue of pregnancy
and work. It found that only around 25 per cent of Australian
businesses provide paid maternity leave, leaving women in an

overwhelming number of workplaces without access to it. According to the report, discrimination on the basis of pregnancy and the lack of access to paid maternity leave are significant factors in women deciding not to have children or limiting the number of children they do have.

More than 120 countries around the world have laws that require the social security system or the employer to pay mothers up to 100 per cent of their wages while they are on maternity leave. In Australia there is paid maternity leave in the public sector, but we do not have laws providing for paid benefits in the private sector, and we do not offer paid maternity leave to most employees who are casual.

Of course, there has been a huge increase in women's participation in the work force over the last few decades. But generally there has been little change in who does the unpaid domestic work at home. We still do not see the value of unpaid domestic work, which is estimated to be around $250 billion, reflected in our formal economic calculations in this country. That's 60 per cent of our gross domestic product not accounted for.

Equal wages, equal opportunities, paid maternity leave, affordable childcare and some recognition for the hours of unpaid labour we do at home: that's what women want. We can all do something to correct these injustices: write letters, lobby our bosses, lobby our unions to treat these issues as of the highest priority. You know what, you could even call your local Member of Parliament. Depending on her childcare arrangements, she just might be able to help you.

This is an edited transcript of a speech Natasha gave at the *marie claire* What Women Want forum on 21 February 2001.

HELEN BARNACLE

After her release from prison Helen Barnacle became a psychologist. She worked in the community sector, as well as singing and songwriting part-time. In 1997 she received an Australia Council Fellowship and wrote her autobiography, *Don't Let Her See Me Cry.* Currently she works as a psychologist, does drama and music with young people in the juvenile justice system, and also does public speaking. Most importantly she is mum to her beautiful daughter, Ali, who is studying at university.

Photograph: Brad Wilson

HELEN BARNACLE

The Frog Who Learnt to Sing

S ome years ago I was asked as part of a workshop to write my life story in the style of a fairytale, but with me as an animal. I cast myself as a frog. Why a frog? Maybe because music and particularly singing have always been a major part of my life, and I love the sound of frogs croaking. The fairytale went something like this.

There was once a little girl frog who had a deep, rich croak and who realised that her croak was a gift. But as she grew up she seemed to always get into trouble when she croaked loudly, and she couldn't understand why other frogs didn't see the beauty of her gift.

'Maybe my croak isn't as deep and rich as I think it is,' she told herself, because it seemed that her gift had become her problem.

The little frog became quieter and quieter until her deep, rich croak was silent. She felt sad, but she hid her sadness too.

Her mother and father rewarded her for her silence because a quiet frog is much less troublesome than an overly expressive frog. This became a way of life for her, and when it came time for her to choose a partner, she chose a male frog that loved her for her silence. It was an easy yet empty relationship because her partner frog was dominating and told her what to do. She didn't question anything, believing that he knew better than she. In all the years they shared he never ever heard her deep, rich croak.

One day, out of sadness and boredom more than anything else, she stood before the mirror and took a long, hard look at herself. She didn't like her reflection, and as she continued to stare into the mirror the pressure of trying to remain silent got too much and she began to blow up. She got bigger and bigger until, just as she was about to burst, she opened her mouth and let out the biggest, deepest, richest sound ever.

She suddenly looked around in fear, afraid someone may have heard her, but nobody had, so she let out another croak and another. She croaked and croaked, her heart brimming with joy, and the next time she looked around her she was surrounded by frogs and they were all smiling. Shocked, she stopped croaking immediately, but they were clapping and cheering and calling out to her to croak some more.

Then the frogs came to her and took her hands, and with her new friends she went leaping, jumping and croaking into the distance. She had found her true frog self.

It's a simple story with a happy ending, as is my human journey through drug addiction and imprisonment. However, the human version isn't as simple, and the terrain has been treacherous and complicated. It has deeper caverns in which

I have sometimes hidden, and darker shadows from which I had to find some sunlight. In the real-life version I fell many times, and met some beautiful people, as well as some ugly and violent ones, along the way. It hasn't been an easy journey, but it is of my own making and, thankfully, I have lived to tell the tale.

I was seventeen when I was introduced to heroin (although I'd already been abusing other drugs and alcohol). I was thirty-one when I had my last hit. I dropped out of school at sixteen and left home soon after. I first went to prison at age twenty-five, got out on bail for a few months, became pregnant, then returned to prison at age twenty-six with my baby daughter, Ali, in my arms. I wasn't released until a couple of weeks before my thirty-fourth birthday in 1987. Ali remained with me in prison until her fourth birthday. She had turned eight by the time I was released.

Ali and I were separated for four interminable years, for the simple reason that I was a heroin addict and, as a result, through my association with others in the drug world, had been sentenced on drug charges. I kept my mouth shut during the trial (there were five of us charged), and have kept my mouth shut ever since. The police offered me an indemnity if I opened my mouth, but I'll never talk to anyone about what really went on back then. I want to live.

I remember clearly when I became confused during adolescence. It was around the time I started secondary school. It was a peculiar feeling, as I'd been extremely successful as a young person. If you can pinpoint a turning point in your life, for me this was it.

At age sixteen and at the beginning of year eleven, after an argument with the principal and vice-principal of the school

I attended, I dropped out. Around the same time, Dad and Mum were having problems, but my brother and I weren't informed, and while my brother supported Mum's silence and submission, I got angry and felt that the whole situation was unfair. I didn't like watching Mum being treated with disrespect, and I couldn't bear the fact that she wouldn't speak up. So I spoke up about it, and it wasn't appreciated.

Increasingly, I was seen as 'the problem', instead of their relationship. Soon my own relationship with my father, which had increasingly deteriorated since I was about thirteen, broke down. That was when I moved out. In fact, on the pretext of starting a professional singing career, I went interstate to get away from all of them.

The problem was, I was insecure and had lost all of that early childhood confidence that I would require to be a performer. While living in Sydney I began using heroin on a regular basis. I was not yet addicted, and initially I thought that heroin restored some of my confidence. I thought it was helping me.

I believe now that after leaving home I went in search of a sense of belonging somewhere else. I found it on the streets among other lost souls – the drug-using community. These people became my friends and I loved them dearly.

Here I found different expectations and priorities to that of the 'real world'. Once addicted to heroin, the major focus in daily life is finding ways to obtain enough money to score the drug. The bottom line is that if you don't get the drug, then you can't function very well, and so your personal goals are reduced almost to this singular purpose – it's an absolute priority. If you don't score then little else happens. The other goals were the usual ones, such as paying the rent, turning up for work on time, and eating at least occasionally. These expectations were vastly different from my previous life, where I'd been sports prefect at school, was always one of the top students academically, and was successful in both my hobbies, callisthenics and classical piano. My singing lessons and daily practice ceased.

In hindsight I wonder, if I'd had someone to talk to about my increasing loss of self-confidence, or if I'd known how to communicate my feelings, could things have turned out differently? Possibly. My advice to any parent or significant other to an adolescent is to keep communication open. Listen to what young people have to say and talk to them about sensitive issues such as sex, drugs, and other risk-taking behaviours, because, developmentally, it's normal for adolescents to experiment with such things. But mostly, help them feel valued. Even if they are behaving rebelliously, they need to feel loved and to have a sense that they belong. If they don't feel that at home, then it's likely they'll go looking for it elsewhere.

I also found a sense of belonging in what turned out to be my most memorable adult lover relationship. Unfortunately, it was a relationship memorable not for the love it brought but for the violence and for the subsequent fear it induced in me.

At the time I thought I was making a better choice of partner because, unlike my previous partner, at least this bloke wasn't a heroin addict. But what I eventually learnt from this relationship was that there are some human beings who are very cruel. This man, who was five years older than I was and aware of my low self-esteem and emotional dependence on him, believed he could treat me any way he liked. He was disrespectful, violent and abusive. So, like the little girl frog and my own mother, I became silent and submissive. It was a situation that continued for many years and became 'normal' to me.

This man spoke to me as though I was worthless. Unfortunately, for many years I believed him. 'You rotten, scumbag junkie! I should have left you in the gutter where I found you!' he would often yell at me. These disgusting words have remained imprinted in my mind, spoken by the man who was supposed to love me. The irony is that if you asked him how he felt about me at the time, he probably would have told you that he did love me, but that I just needed to be slapped into obedience.

How did I meet him? He was my dealer. He initially gave me access to the drug that I craved above all else – heroin. The drug was more important to me than a lover, but I preferred to have both. I'd buy heroin, use some myself and sell the rest to friends. My friends did the same for me. Then we'd repeat the sequence later that day, and the same the next day. It was difficult, because I also had a straight job as a receptionist, so this activity was restricted to outside my work hours, which meant all night every night.

Some months later, after I became involved with this particular dealer, he wouldn't allow me to use heroin. It turned out that, actually, he thought all junkies were scumbags. He was merely a heroin dealer, not a heroin addict. Daily, he would threaten to kill me if he caught me using heroin. But this couldn't stop me using the drug. Later on, my brother's love and support couldn't stop me; giving birth to my most precious daughter couldn't stop me. Back then, I was unable to 'decide' to stop using because, for a variety of reasons, I wasn't ready to stop, even though at different stages throughout my heroin-using years I thought I was finished with the drug. I overdosed several times, but it never occurred to me that I could actually die.

I have often asked myself: 'How come I survived? Why didn't I die?' So many of my friends didn't survive their heroin-using years. So many of my friends died of overdoses before they reached thirty. They were equally as weak or strong as I was, depending on your perspective. Why do some live and others die? Why can't people stop using when their backs are up against the wall? Why does it seem to have to get so desperately bad before someone can make the change? I don't know all the answers, but in my case it became a question of choosing to live or die, rather than trying to give up heroin.

This point came for me about halfway through my sentence, during my fourth and fifth years inside. I was so depressed that I became suicidal. The depression was prompted by my separation from my daughter, Ali, then four. I can't remember whether this period of time lasted for weeks or months, but it seemed like a black, bleak forever.

At the time I wrote some notes in my diary about the fear I was feeling and the lack of motivation to keep on going.

Fear – not wanting to get out of bed in the morning. Not wanting to walk to the shower, feeling like no matter how long I showered for I couldn't cleanse myself. Not wanting to walk out of my cell, not wanting to see the day, not wanting to see anybody, not wanting to hear any voices, not wanting to live any more. Being afraid to go on living 'cause I couldn't bear the pain of it any more, afraid it wouldn't change – afraid I couldn't change – it or me. Afraid of the years ahead without Ali. Afraid of never being loved again, afraid of never loving anyone again, afraid of not being Ali's mum again. Afraid of using; afraid of not using. Afraid of feeling. Afraid my brother wouldn't ever accept me again. Afraid of being straight – what would that mean? How do you feel as a straight person? How do you behave?

I felt so distraught my whole body ached, and for the first time since I began using heroin, it couldn't kill the pain. During the hours I was locked in my cell, I'd pass the time thinking up ways to kill myself. I didn't want to feel anything any more because it hurt too much.

Around this time (I was about thirty-one), I found myself at the crossroads, but I couldn't move forward and I couldn't go back. I was stuck – suicidal, vulnerable, broken. My heroin addiction was a major issue because it kept me dependent and it kept me powerless. It also kept me in trouble because it was illegal. I was sick of feeling worthless. At this point, I cared about nothing except Ali. There were only two choices left for me:

1. Kill myself – this would provide relief to me and everyone else, except Ali.
2. Live – this would be good for Ali (at least I believed so).

But if I chose to live I had to find a way to like myself as an independent human being, not just in my role as a mother. I had to find some peace inside instead of the resident torment.

Perhaps the only reason I didn't choose to die was that I wanted so much to be Ali's mum in the future. That experience had given me such love and joy in the past. Being separated from Ali in the present was killing me. I was not only dependent, but also grief-stricken.

I wrote about my heroin addiction in my diary. I was five years into my sentence and still psychologically addicted to heroin, although not physically:

Why I use:

I use because it kills the pain inside – it's a pain killer! It fills up that big vacant hole inside. I don't know why I feel like I've got a big hole inside, but smack is the only thing that's filled the hole, made me feel warm inside, even if it is only momentarily.

You can't fix a problem if you don't know what the problem is. I've been told I'm the problem, but I don't feel like I'm a problem, or bad, or mean, or nasty or anything like that. I don't hurt people, I only hurt myself, and I only hurt myself because I don't care about myself. I care about some people that are close to me, but I don't give a shit about me because I'm nothing really. Take away my daughter and there's nothing left because there is no me. I'm an empty shell. She's the only thing I have that's worth something. When I look at her I feel love and warmth, I feel proud to have her and she's mine, she came from me, but take her away and I want to hide 'cause there is no me. I have no substance.

I don't know how to talk about these things. Who could I tell? They'd think I was mad and put me in a psychiatric hospital. But I'm not mad. I just don't like me, I don't know me, and I don't know how to tell anyone.

So don't take my daughter away, 'cause there'll be nothing left. Sometimes I wish I was invisible so I could see everyone but they couldn't see me. Then I wouldn't feel like hiding all the time.

Reading these words still produces a body memory of that time, and my heart feels heavy. It's hard to believe now that I felt so worthless, and it's still difficult to read what I wrote all those years ago, but the memory remains so strong it lives in my bones. I don't read these notes very often, it's just too sad.

It's obvious that I had extremely low self-esteem, but I still didn't believe I was a bad person, just a troubled one. From my teenage years onward that's how I'd felt, but I didn't have the knowledge and guidance to know what to do about it. Prison didn't offer anything by way of assistance either – just more punishment.

I had to discover where and how to start changing. Assistance is often found in the strangest places, and the best help I received was from my music teacher in the prison education centre. He was a Buddhist, and he taught me some techniques to utilise. I began to meditate, and slowly, slowly, I began to be able to fill my heart with love and compassion, replacing the angst and self-doubt.

Sometimes now people comment on how 'strong and courageous' I am. When I was a heroin user, nobody would have said I was a strong and courageous person, with one exception perhaps. Then a teacher in the education centre told me I was strong. She told me that many times, and I'm glad she said it, but the odds were against my believing it. I felt weak and helpless, and I knew that society saw all of us in prison as weak, defective human beings. This belief was reinforced by many, perhaps most, of the prison officers. Even by my own standards I was a failure.

At one point during my heroin-using days when I was still in prison my brother had considered taking custody of my daughter, merely because I was still using heroin, not because

I was a bad mother. Back then, there was little access to drug education and information, and he wrongly assumed that I couldn't be a competent mother. I was, and I knew it, but I couldn't have convinced anyone else of that. Except, once again, that teacher, because she saw me with Ali in the education centre on a daily basis. The other exception would be my co-prisoners. They wouldn't have judged me either, because they also shared a beautiful relationship with Ali. My daughter made the prison a more humane place for a while.

About a year after my diary notes on fear and using, I somehow found the motivation to change. Largely that motivation grew out of despair.

I was living in 'cottage 6' in the medium-security section of the prison. Here we lived in little houses with four bedrooms and, unlike the maximum security section where you were locked in your cell every night, while the cottage itself was locked at 4.30 pm, the bedrooms remained unlocked. In my attempt to feel better about myself I had begun to practise daily the meditation techniques taught to me by my Buddhist friend. During meditation I would open my heart and connect with Ali, who was now living with my brother, Ron. I'd send out love to her – it helped me to feel close to her when I couldn't physically be there. I always commenced or finished my meditation this way.

Now, while I was still physically locked up in a prison, I was able to free my psyche in a way that I hadn't felt since childhood. But something else was also happening. The breathing and focusing was creating a change. I was beginning to feel strong and unafraid. I knew deep inside that I was finished with using heroin. I knew I didn't need it any more. I had learnt how to say no. I had observed myself saying no. I heard myself saying no. I had never felt so strong. I knew that now I could do anything. I now felt motivated to live instead of to die.

I started doing physical exercise daily, which made me feel healthy and more alert. I had learnt that ceasing heroin use was only the initial part of the journey; that what followed was an emotional quest, which would actually continue for the rest of my life.

I let go of most of my previous drug-using attitudes and beliefs, particularly the belief that I was useless and worthless. Only those people who were important to me remained in my life. It was like there was nothing else around me. I had to become very self-focused for a time, but I was determined to change the way I thought and lived. Really, I was fighting for my life. I was content in that room inside cottage 6, peaceful for the first time in years.

My link to the future was Ali. I still had a couple of years of my sentence to serve before we could be reunited, but with that link in place, I felt there was a possibility of feeling happiness. I felt safe knowing that a future with Ali was possible, that Ron would never prevent that. I now believed that he would never try to take Ali from me. It was like the sky had opened up and I could do anything, achieve anything. Nothing would stop me.

I did a great deal of personal development in my last couple of years in prison, mostly based on Buddhist philosophy. I also studied psychology. So when I was released from prison I felt strong and self-assured, but I was quite naive about how society works – the structures, both formal and informal, that exist within the community. It was during the first year after my release from prison, while observing my brother and the few straight friends I had, that I realised 'normal' people don't have it all together, either, that they struggle and they behave in ways that are hurtful and insensitive, and that some 'normals' have as many problems as I ever had! This was a revelation, as I'd come to believe that somehow I was born different to these people. I had always felt as if I had two heads, and that when people looked at me they could see I was different to them. It took me some years to learn how to fit into the normal world and realise that I was unique but no different to others around me. I came to wish I'd known this fact all those years ago.

It's futile to think of drug addiction in terms of mounting a 'war on drugs', as politicians and the media regularly suggest. People who develop behaviours such as drug or alcohol addiction, eating disorders or gambling addictions, are very often people just like you and me. Many develop dependent or addictive behaviours through a loss of self-esteem or confidence, or through a sense that they have no community to which they can belong. Locking people away from a problem doesn't solve it. Troubled, lonely or alienated people need help and inclusion, not punishment. Self-respect is hard to gain when the world is against you.

And so the next time you hear a frog croak, think of me, because I am one of the lucky ones. Like the little girl frog, I am alive, I believe I'm worthwhile, and I feel like I belong. I've also found my voice.

ZOE CARIDES

Zoe Carides has acted in films, television and theatre for twenty years. During that time she has written, recorded and performed songs, exhibited her paintings, had a few pieces of writing published and brought up a child. She spends a great deal of time driving.

ZOE CARIDES

A Mother of a Job

I 'm of the opinion that we're all just animals, really. You know us women: at a certain point in our lives we suddenly hear Cornelia Frances in our heads saying, 'Start the clock', and from there it's a steady and desperate race to climb to the top of our profession, sustain a meaningful relationship, keep love handles at bay, laugh lines to a bare minimum – and have a baby.

I so wanted to be a mother. I was ready. Ready for my whole life to be changed. Ready to face morning sickness, ready to face the swelling of my belly. (I wasn't too keen about the swelling of my butt but that comes with pregnancy.) I was a little scared of labour but human pregnancy is designed to acclimatise you to the idea, because by the time you've been in the pregnant state for about forty weeks you're going, 'Get this thing out of here!'

Giving birth to my daughter was the most incredible thing

I've ever done, that's without a doubt. The contractions that squeezed her into this world were like tidal waves of agony. The pain of labour is big. It's the Grand Canyon of pains: it's sweeping and majestic, and it brings you to your knees, literally.

I was thirty when I became a mother and I was actually one of the youngest in my birth class. Women are choosing to have babies later these days, and some women are choosing not to become mothers at all, which I think is a very wise and loving choice, because you know there ain't no point in having them if you don't really want them. Because it's hard work and it's constant work. It's also intensely loving work.

I remember going to a function shortly after I'd had my daughter, Paris, and running into a colleague of mine. 'So, how's motherhood coming along? How's it going?' he asked me.

'Oh, it's incredible,' I said. 'I can't believe that women have been doing this job for centuries and they've never been *paid* to do it. I mean this is like a full-time job, it makes a filming day look like a picnic. A filming day *ends*! This is constant. You're up through the night. You're on call twenty-four hours a day.'

'You shouldn't have a baby if you don't want to do all that stuff,' he said sagely.

'Oh no, I'm not saying that,' I said. 'I'm just saying it's incredible. It's the hardest work I've ever done. It's the most rewarding work I've ever done, but I'm just saying, you know, I've only got one. My mother had three. How did she do it?'

Anyway, I love my daughter like crazy. Where are the cameras so I can say, 'I love you Paris, I love you Paris.' She's one of the most articulate, funny, intelligent and caring people that I have ever met. I can also get angrier with her than with anyone else I know. She really pushes my buttons, but hey, that's fun because who else was going to teach me all those valuable lessons.

The first weeks of motherhood are a total blur for most women. Even so, there's an expectation that a woman delivers a baby then looks like a highly paid Hollywood actress within three weeks. But that's just not going to happen, because most of us don't have personal trainers to whip our arses into shape, or nannies to do the glorious three-hourly nightly feeds for a few months (if you're very conscientious about breastfeeding).

So most of us just struggle through the first year of child rearing as best we can with no real blueprint for how to parent. We just get by on scraps of information that we glean from other parents in supermarket queues or playgrounds or the 24-hour help line at Tresillian which, just quietly, received an awful lot of calls from me during that first year.

All the while we're terrified of turning into our own mothers. Oh no, we're not going to say the things to our kids that our mothers said to us, are we? No, no. But then, one by one, Mother's Greatest Hits are trotted out, including the smash singles 'I'll Give You Something to Really Cry About' and 'How Many Times Do I Have to Tell You?'.

But all these problems don't really seem like problems if I stop to consider the countless women in the world who want to be mothers but can't for some reason. Those to whom it's been decreed by some power that they shalt not conceive. Or women who actually were mothers, who had a child, and that child died or was taken from them. What about them? They're still mothers. I'm sure those women would give anything to hear whingeing and whining about the house. And because I know that the pain of these women exists in the world, it reminds me every day to be grateful for the job that I've been given and for the honour of being my daughter's mother.

Yes, we do want motherhood, most of us. But I want to know why motherhood is not revered in our society as it should be. Raising a human being is one of the most important jobs you can do and yet there is not much recognition for it. Motherhood is a very, very challenging job. But there's no paid maternity leave. There's no sick leave, no holiday pay, no holiday, really. There's no pay rise as the job gets harder and requires more skill over the years.

Still, we want to be excellent mothers, tirelessly giving and endlessly patient and providing three solid meals a day that include at least four out of the five food groups. But, you know, these days we also want to be brilliant careerists and conscientious recyclists. We also want to try to be sexual beings for our partners. (Oh, by the way, partners, husbands, if you do believe in a sex life after children, just do some housework regularly without being asked. Because nothing closes a woman's legs faster than resentment.)

Most of us just try and do the best we can, and when we need help we turn to our families if we can. We turn to our friends and lean on them. And the other thing that mothers do is turn to other mothers. The parents of our child's friends at school. We don't always know these women very well – we may not hang out with them socially. We might just have a few quick exchanges in the playground after school. But we really rely on these women and we rely on each other as mothers.

Because motherhood unites women. Even women who aren't mothers are united by motherhood, because we're all daughters, and as your mother's daughter you carry her story within you. And united, we might just be able to achieve what it is that women want. First, recognition that being a mother is just about the most important job anyone can do, and we want some paid maternity leave as part of that recognition. And if we can't each have a personal trainer after the birth, or a wet nurse for the nightly feeds, at the very least we want some help with the housework and the chance every now and then to have a good lie down.

This is an edited transcript of a speech Zoe gave at the *marie claire* What Women Want forum on 10 October 2001.

PHOEBE FRASER

Phoebe Fraser is studying international law. For the last four years she has been a representative on the National Council for the Centenary of Federation. Previously Phoebe worked for eight years for CARE Australia, distributing supplies to flood victims in Bangladesh and famine victims in Somalia, co-ordinating emergency centres for lost and orphaned Rwandan children and leading the CARE International Assessment mission to Bosnia-Herzegovina. Her book *A Single Seed* was published in 1996. Phoebe lives in Melbourne with her husband and two sons.

PHOEBE FRASER

One Small Voice

In 1992 there was famine in Somalia. By then I had already been working for CARE Australia for three years, in Thailand, Cambodia, Bangladesh, Iran, Iraq, Geneva, Angola and Zimbabwe. But due to the intense media interest in Somalia I suddenly found myself in the public eye.

Since that time it seems that people continue to be slightly mystified by how a western district girl and daughter of a former prime minister ended up in a place like Somalia. The simple answer is this: each of us can make a difference. We all do it in different ways. Some have the gift of laughter, others a green thumb. Every contribution makes the world a rich, vibrant and interesting place. Some of us fall into our niche, others spend a lifetime looking. A love of Africa and great good fortune led me to mine.

Recently I have been reading Dr Seuss to my children. He sums it up beautifully in *Horton Hears a Who*. In that story the kangaroo and monkeys are preparing to destroy a clover, but Horton the elephant tells them that an entire village is living there. Horton can hear the 'Whos' who live on the clover but the other animals can't, and they think he's gone mad. Horton entreats the Whos to speak up as loudly as they can, for if they can make themselves heard they will be safe. They do, but the mayor of the Who village finds one tiny Who who has failed to raise his voice. The mayor begs the little Who to help and finally, the young lad shouts 'Yopp'. Dr Seuss writes:

> *That one small, extra Yopp put it over!*
> *Finally, at last! From that speck on that clover*
> *Their voices were heard! They rang out clear and clean.*
> *And the elephant smiled. 'Do you see what I mean? . . .*
> *They've proved they ARE persons, no matter how small.*
> *And their whole world was saved by the Smallest of All!'*

While I never had delusions about saving whole worlds, I joined CARE Australia in 1989 because I felt that injustices needed to be addressed and I believed strongly that existing inequalities in the world were not only unjust but unsustainable.

My view that something could and must be done was buoyed by the optimism that marked the beginning of the 1990s. The cold war had ended and the United Nations (UN) appeared to be finding its feet as a force for good in the world. So when famine struck Somalia, while it appeared to be a famine like any other its global impact was quite different.

The Somali crisis came on the heels of the success of the

Gulf War, which saw the UN take action against an aggressor state. United States President George Bush hailed the beginning of a New World Order, creating an atmosphere of optimism and hope. It was thought that from now on justice could prevail. Certainly a famine of the proportions of that in Somalia could not be tolerated. International action had saved Kuwait; it could also save Somalia. The international community responded.

The response was significant. It was the first time the UN Security Council had enacted special powers to intervene in another state for humanitarian purposes. For the first time the international community had got together and said, this is not good enough, we're not going to let these people starve to death, even if we have to use force to prevent it. This was significant because it broke one of the most fundamental tenets of the UN Charter, that of sovereign integrity and non-interference in the domestic jurisdiction of a member state. Yet it was a change for the best. The humanitarian intervention in Somalia was a statement by the international community that human suffering cannot be tolerated, wherever it is found, and that we can all do something about it.

When I arrived there were over 400 people dying every day, but with the increased aid effort we soon saw the humanitarian situation turned around and the light returned to the children's eyes. Communities went back to their villages to sow crops in time for the harvest. Life began to return to normal.

But while the humanitarian situation in Somalia improved the UN failed to address the economic and political chaos that dominated the situation. The international force had undertaken to disarm Somali militias, but there were no programs put in place to retrain the militias and clansmen and provide them with gainful employment. These men had only survived the previous few years by the strength of their weapons and their preparedness to use them. To take those weapons away and provide nothing in return doomed the international intervention to failure.

By the end of the first quarter of 1993 the situation had begun to deteriorate again. Two American Black Hawk helicopters were shot down over Mogadishu and an American serviceman was dragged through the streets. America's support for the UN operation was withdrawn and Operation Restore Hope came to a close.

In eight short months events in Somalia had given enormous hope to the international community and had taken it away again. The UN's fatal error was to have no real plan to resolve the political impasse in Somalia. Yet the entire process was not new. At the same time as Somalia was collapsing, the UN was reconstructing the political face of Cambodia with remarkable success. A similar UN interim administration in Somalia may have provided longer-term solutions to that country's problems.

The UN's failure in Somalia in 1993 brought into question what was really meant by 'New World Order'. Perhaps it was not going to be as easy to solve the world's problems as was thought in those early and in some ways heady days of the post–cold war era. And in many ways the failure in Somalia was responsible in the years that followed for other notable international failures, such as the lack of UN action in Bosnia and Rwanda. Certainly in the case of Rwanda, UN member states did not want to be involved in what they saw as another unresolvable African conflict.

However, throughout the 1990s the UN became increasingly active. The Security Council, unhindered by the cold war, was able to use its special powers to invoke change around the globe and increasingly did so. The world was becoming a smaller place and there was a growing involvement at an international level in the domestic affairs of states.

Globalisation is the catchword used for the altered political and economic environment that faces us in the new millennium. Communications technology has meant that information and knowledge are more accessible than ever before. We are all aware of what is happening around the globe. For better or worse, this has resulted in more involvement and more action than ever before.

Critics of globalisation see it as a function of big business, where governments have less and less influence in the market place and in many ways less influence on the future of their constituents. They say profit is the new God. As a result, they argue, businesses have often shifted dirty industries to third world countries in order to reduce costs and avoid environmental regulations at home. Child labour and sweat shops are common places of origin of the luxury goods we find in our supermarkets and boutiques.

Therefore, we should question how the power of big business affects our democracies and the unrepresentative nature of business, which makes decisions that directly affect our futures. But we also need to weigh up the opportunities that globalisation presents.

Imagine a woman in Bangladesh being able to telephone the market to find out the real prices for rice on a certain day, thereby reducing the opportunity for the middle man to exploit those out of touch with the market. Or an African villager going to a touch screen for simple medical advice.

The influence of international human rights agreements is increasing. Governments and tyrants can no longer get away with murder without fear of prosecution. This is a significant advance in many ways attributable to globalisation.

From an aid worker's point of view, through globalisation we may now truly come to grips with the fact that we live in a world where 80 per cent of the population exist in poverty. It's a world where environmental destruction continues in many countries because their only economy is based on the consumption of natural resources; where children still die of diseases that are preventable; and where the countries hardest hit by the AIDS epidemic are unable to access drugs because of intellectual property laws.

Although this all seems a long way away, thanks to globalisation we can no longer ignore it. If we are to maintain our lifestyles and way of life in the future the challenge now is to address these disparities. There is no reason why the majority of the world's population should watch the rich get richer while they struggle to feed their children.

We need to engage in the wider global community with humanity and compassion. International human rights standards have been put in place and treaties signed in an effort to protect people from daily violations. We should honour and protect those treaties. It's in all our interests to do so.

In Australia we are facing important human rights challenges, particularly with regard to the situation of refugees in detention centres. In many ways, of equal concern are the lack of compassion in public discussion about refugees in Australia, and the apparent lack of understanding about from where the refugees have come. It's easy to ignore and condemn those for whom we have little understanding. Their experiences are so far from our own.

But imagine, just for a moment, that you feel so desperate, so without hope or trust in the future, that you are prepared to rise up from your chair, throw a couple of things into a shoulder bag and walk out the door. If you're lucky you might have transport but more likely you will be travelling by foot. You gather your family around you but your eldest son is still at school. Should you jeopardise everyone for his sake? Do you have time to pass by the school and collect him? Will he be there or will the school have been evacuated? You look into the eyes of your partner and younger son and daughter and make the decision to go directly to the border. If you can save the majority of your family you will be lucky.

As you walk out of your street, your suburb, your town, and head towards the nearest border, crowds are gathering about you. A neighbour is wheeling his ancient mother in a wheelbarrow while he carries his infant on his back. The walk is long and arduous so you guard carefully the water and food you have brought with you. Finally you reach a refugee camp where you hope there will be someone to help you. Your food has run out, you are tired, and one of your children has fallen ill on the journey.

Gradually you fall into a routine in the camp. You are given a place to set up your piece of plastic sheeting – the only shelter you will have. You have been given your rations for the next two weeks – maize, beans, a little sugar, oil and salt. Now there is little to do but wait for things to change, wait to go home.

In Iran, 1.2 million refugees were in camps at the end of the Gulf War. At the time I was struck by how, in our efforts to meet the physical needs of the refugees, we tended to forget the trauma they had suffered, the experiences they'd had on the road to their appalling destination and the subsequent effect on their lives.

One man told me that as they fled to Iran his three-month-old daughter became ill and died. The earth was frozen solid and they had neither the time nor the tools to stop and bury her. As they crossed a fast-flowing river he said a prayer with his wife and left the baby, tightly swaddled, to be swept away to a watery burial downstream. How could we ever measure the impact of such an experience? These are not the decisions anyone takes lightly. They are not situations we would choose to be in.

There is not only the trauma of the flight from danger, but also the trauma of daily existence: the boredom of daily life in the camps; the humiliation of being totally dependent. The effects can be severe and long-term, ranging from the general retardation of children's development to depression in adults. In the camps in Iran the men had an advantage as they could gather together at the temporary mosque, spend time together and talk about the Koran and life in general. But there was no focal point or equivalent support network for women.

The issue of refugees is a potent one in Australia at the moment. These men, women and children who are so desperate they give up everything to get on a dreadful sinking hulk find themselves labelled 'queue jumpers'. What I can say is that in no refugee camp that I have ever been in was there a queue for third-party asylum. In no camp I have been in was there a clear view to a better future. I can't blame the asylum seekers for trying to come any way they can. When there is no hope, no alternative to the dreadful monotony and desperation of a camp but a slim possibility of freedom and a better way of life, I know which choice I would make.

I would take a chance at life in a country that has an extraordinary record for democracy, freedom and a rich and fortunate way of life. A country that has had a reputation for generosity of spirit, which has welcomed refugees and immigrants by their hundreds of thousands in the past – a country built on immigration.

We are told that the policies on refugees put forward by the government and supported (until recently) by the opposition simply reflect public opinion. In response to that I would like to quote the Right Honourable Lord Bingham of Cornhill, the Lord Chief Justice of England and Wales, who noted that while parliament has responsibility for the ultimate protection of those under its jurisdiction, by its very nature parliament has an interest in maintaining the support of the electorate. As a result, it is possible 'to identify a number of groups who have been either unpopular or disregarded and whose rights and freedoms have as a result been of little or no parliamentary interest: Jews, Roman Catholics, dissenters; vagrants, vagabonds, beggars, gypsies, married women; children; prisoners; mental patients, and the disabled; immigrants of various kinds, asylum seekers, aliens; homosexuals, strikers; single mothers . . .' He goes on to note that 'Public Opinion is an unreliable source of protection to those most in need of it'. It is possible that the desperate asylum seekers perilously reaching our shores are victims of such 'protection'.

What we need to remember is that there is no future for any of us, refugees or not, in a world of inequities and grave injustice. There is no hope for any sort of New World Order when gross disparities between rich and poor are tolerated and human rights are violated. If we are prepared to recognise the need for a global approach to human issues – so Somalis are not left to starve while richer nations leave subsidised land fallow, so weak and strong nations alike have obligations, so human beings are protected from the vagaries of governments and power – then we have to strive towards that end. We have to raise our voices and defend our beliefs. We have to be prepared to work for a better world and not leave the hard yakka to someone else.

I am an individualist. I believe that every contribution can make a difference, no matter how small. I have faith in the little Who from Dr Seuss whose one small voice among thousands rang out and tipped the scale between survival and destruction.

TRACEY CURRO

Tracey Curro has worked in commercial television for over fifteen years. After graduating from the Queensland University of Technology she worked as a news reporter and prime time news presenter before joining 'Beyond 2000' and then '60 Minutes'. Recently, working with her husband Michael Rivette, Tracey has co-produced and co-written the documentaries *Somebody's Mother*, on ovarian cancer, and *Xanana*, on the East Timorese resistance leader's path to the presidency. Tracey is thirty-eight, married, with one child.

Photograph: Robert Piccoli

TRACEY CURRO

Walking in the Shoes of the
Women of Suai

I f all women have a universal desire it must surely be for freedom from violence and for peace, security and a future for our children. But until recently the women of East Timor lived with oppression, violence and the prospect of a bleak future for their children. And in September 1999 East Timor was razed to the ground during a fortnight of un-imaginable violence. It seems that mankind's capacity for destruction and evil knows no bounds (and I say *man*kind deliberately here!).

Now the people of East Timor face the task of rebuilding a new nation from the ashes of the old. I feel enormously privileged as a journalist to have won the consent and co-operation of Xanana Gusmao and his Australian wife, Kirsty Sword, to document East Timor's transition to a free and democratic society. But after 450 years of colonial rule by

Portugal and twenty-four years of oppressive occupation by Indonesian forces many East Timorese understand the concept of democracy only as a freedom they have continually been denied. Therefore, one step along the road to national elections has been a program of civic education, which has explained what democracy is, how a democracy functions and the role and responsibilities of the people in a democratic society.

The task that lies ahead for the new nation of East Timor is daunting. But the friendship and support of the world community – including people like each and every one of us here – can and does make a real difference to the lives of the East Timorese.

To help make a difference I co-chair a community-based group called Friends of Suai, which was set up in Melbourne's city of Port Phillip. Suai was the scene of one of the worst massacres committed during the violence that followed East Timor's ballot for independence. Two hundred people died in the church in Suai that day – 6 September 1999 – including three priests. Port Phillip has entered into a ten-year partnership with Suai to rebuild the town and to help rebuild the lives of its people.

It was on a visit to Suai to honour and commemorate the victims of that tragedy that I met Elizeu, his beautiful 24-year-old wife, Maria, and their four-year-old son, Eric. On the day of the Suai massacre, Elizeu saw things he can never forget and still now struggles to forgive. Hiding in the bushes the 27-year-old saw militiamen surround the church and murder his friends and neighbours. He saw priests shot dead or hacked with machetes. He saw bodies, twenty at least, piled up and burned in front of the church. When at last it was dark he escaped through the bush and into the mountains.

His wife and son had hidden in the nuns' dormitory. They were captured and taken away. Then, day after day, while the little boy stood outside the room, soldiers and militiamen queued up and repeatedly raped the young woman, until her hips were dislocated and she could no longer walk.

Recently, Fokupers, the largest women's group in East Timor, revealed the existence of 'rape houses' across the country, including in Suai, houses in which women were held to be used as chattels by Indonesian military officers. Fokupers calls the women once held in these houses 'survivors'. Not victims, survivors. To date, their database includes the testimony of more than 200 women raped in the name of war.

Kirsty Sword has sought to publicise the plight of one such woman, also from Suai, although Juliana dos Santos is barely a woman. She was a fifteen-year-old girl when she was kidnapped in September 1999 and taken across the border into West Timor. Paraded pregnant along the border between east and west, this young girl became a trophy, a spoil of war. Juliana gave birth to the baby of her captor, the same man who killed her brother in front of her. Juliana's parents maintain their hope that she will one day come home.

Women's groups are working to meet the many needs of East Timor's women, setting up shelters, trauma counselling centres and training and education programs, addressing maternal and infant health, and playing an important advocacy role. In a nation where 80 per cent of the population live a subsistence existence, poverty and tradition have conspired to keep women oppressed. Gender inequity is ingrained in East Timorese culture. Therefore, women's groups are preaching the message of gender equity, but it takes time to change the attitudes and cultural beliefs that continue to disadvantage women.

I love what I do for a living. It is a tremendous privilege to be allowed into people's lives in an intimate and honest way, to be granted custodianship of their stories and their experiences, to witness events, to see how people respond. We are each unique, and yet we share a universal emotional terrain. It is this that motivates humanitarian work, when we can put ourselves in another person's shoes and understand how that person must feel.

But with all the people and all the injustice in the world that competes for our attention these days, why East Timor? Why care? To answer that question, let's take a moment to reflect on a little history. First, remember that 40 000 East Timorese died fighting with Australian troops during World War II. Remember how the Australian government rushed to grant legitimacy to Indonesia's invasion of East Timor – all because of oil rights in the Timor Sea. Remember that five Australian journalists were killed in East Timor during that 1975 invasion. At the very least, remember that thousands of East Timorese died because they would not be subdued by the Indonesian military.

No, it wasn't our fault. But we can recognise that decisions taken in the past by our political leaders in our interests have had a crushing and tragic impact on the people who are our neighbours and we can act accordingly.

Remember the people who still have no homes, the children who don't yet have a school to go to, the women who gave up their husbands and sons to the struggle, the memories that families like Elizeu, Maria and Eric do not deserve but cannot erase. And think, there but for the grace of God go I.

A portion of the money raised tonight will go directly to the women of Suai. So just by being here you have already helped improve a woman's life in some small way. Thank you.

This is an edited transcript of a speech Tracey gave at the *marie claire* What Women Want forum on 21 February 2001.

SARAH MACDONALD

Sarah Macdonald is a journalist, broadcaster and commentator. She's best
known as the presenter of the 'Morning
Show' on Triple J and several shows on
ABC TV. Sarah returned from overseas
in May 2002 and her first book, *Holy
Cow – An Indian Adventure,* chronicles her
travels. She now presents 'Bush Telegraph' on Radio National.

SARAH MACDONALD

A Guilt-ridden Love Affair

bsence indeed makes the heart grow fonder. For more than two years while living in India I've been immersed in a one-sided yet increasingly passionate long-distance love affair. From afar I've fallen deeper and deeper in love with Australia.

I've pined and yearned for huge skies, rough seas and down-to-earth compatriots. I've bored my Indian friends with tales about Sydney's glittering harbour, crescent-moon beaches and fantastic fresh food. I've even had erotic dreams about green bushland and the red dust of the top end. I've romanticised my country and my compatriots as only a long-distance lover can.

I've been living in New Delhi, the most polluted city on earth with a population almost as large as Australia's. It's dry, dusty and diesel dark; it's noisy, crowded and intense; it's either horrifically hot or smoggy freezing. In short, it's infuriatingly awful. For thirty months I didn't see the sea or any blue sky and I lost the lightness of being that the space, silence and solitude of the Australian landscape bred into my blood. Not that I gave New Delhi much of a chance. I never even considered giving my heart to my temporary home; I was faithful to Australia.

But the danger in long-distance romance is that it forgives and forgets a true love's faults. It freezes the lover in the heart as something perfect, timeless and changeless. I only began to wonder whether my lovely country would actually be the home I'd fantasised about when I finally packed up my South-Asian life and prepared to return to Australia.

I grew nervous about the love reunion. All the familiar relationship questions went through my head. What if I've changed? What if Australia has changed? Will it work? Do we still have enough in common? What if Australia doesn't want me?

Still, when I arrived home, I was so happy to be reunited with my long-yearned-for love, I kissed the ground at Sydney airport. But now I'm back I'm finding that it's not all high passion. In fact, I'm amidst a reunion with a lover that's not at all what I had worshipped from afar.

Sure, I'm on a happy high that only a true love can give. But it's a guilty pleasure. Life here seems too luxurious and too well guarded. While newspapers talk about overcrowding and a 'full city' I marvel at open empty streets and space in which to frolic. Australia doesn't seem full to me any more.

Or, obviously, to our federal government – it has announced it will slightly increase immigration numbers to allow up to 110 000 migrants into our country next year. But it has changed its policy on what sort of people can come. The numbers of business migrants and skilled new Australians will increase at the expense of refugees. We will only keep 12 000 spots for those most desperate for protection and a better life.

In some ways I agree with this decision. It makes good economic sense – it earns us more money and should cost us less. But a part of me is uncomfortable with the equation. Is it fair to take so few when poorer countries are taking so many? What does it say about Australia? What does it say about me? And this increase in spending on 'border protection' and a 'pacific solution' sounds ominous in its terminology.

So my blind adoration for Australia has been tempered by reality. And my affection for India has blossomed. Certainly while I was there India flirted with me: it flattered me with attention until I slowly warmed to its attractive qualities, and it bestowed me with gifts.

The biggest gift India gave me was instant: it made me realise how lucky I was to have been born a middle-class Aussie. But its other great gift was one that just kept on coming. It was that, despite living in a crowded land of one billion people, Indians were endlessly willing to share their lives, their homes, their hearts and their country with me.

I'll never forget spending a baking-hot, 43-degree weekend in the countryside. I was staying in an expensive palace hotel that towered over a struggling village. At six in the morning I sweated down the path to the local well that doubled as a communal bathhouse and was the centre of village life.

Chattering children and smiling adults immediately surrounded me and welcomed my presence. Indian people are fascinated by foreignness and we talked easily, despite the language difficulties. When the school bell rang and the men set off to work a young girl took my hand. She led me to the home she shared with her mother, father, grandparents and five brothers and sisters, a tiny, square, blue concrete house with dirt floors and tin cigarette posters for art.

Soon twenty local village women filed in to meet the stranger. They sat me on a string charpoy bed, squatted at my feet and offered me food, tea and a bed for the night. They told me about their marriage parties and their husbands, their children and their grandparents, their fields and their failures. They even asked me to name the village's most recent addition, a tiny brown baby girl floppy with heat and sticky with sweat.

This type of exchange was not unique. From big cities to tiny villages I've fielded endless offers of chai, chats and charpoy beds and I've barged right into homes, offices, slums and gardens and never caused offence. If I asked directions from one person six would stop and offer to help. In most of India people would approach me wanting to talk, touch, stare and take my photo – I'm on mantelpieces all over the country and I'm still getting postcards from people who just wanted to write to a 'friend' from another land. At first this constant attention was often aggravating but as I became used to it I increasingly felt like a welcomed and valued guest.

India doesn't just find room for temporary residents such as I. It also somehow finds space for thousands of Tibetan

worst of the world has always been there to some degree. But it's up to our leaders to appeal to the best in us, to try to draw out certain characteristics that will help our society and each other. Instead, Australia's leadership seems to be trying to appeal to our smallness of spirit, our fear of others. During the election it seemed to enjoy sucking out our meanness and spitting it back in our face. And I'm not just talking about how we deal with refugees.

In Australia we also try to keep our poor at a distance; I can escape poverty here in a way I couldn't in India. And Sydney seems more obsessed with money than New Delhi. This city is awash with talk about interest rates and mortgages and buying a little space that's yours. I'm trying to hang on to what I learnt in India – that I am rich and privileged and what matters most in life is good health and love. But I can feel the virus of envy and greed seeping through my pores. Multiplying and pumping through my veins and coursing through my heart is a renewed desire for Real Estate.

What's also worrying is that my rising obsession leaves little time or room for a sense of charity. I simply don't have the time for people that I did in India. I'm back into work mode, where a career defines my identity and my worth to society, back to working long days and trying to fit in living around a job. It seems hard to find spare time to care for sick friends, be with my nieces or clean the garden for an aging aunt. When I do get around to these tiny 'good deeds' it's hard not to feel some resentment. Already I am so wrapped up in my own desires and fears of not being able to keep up with the Joneses, I'm growing concerned I can't care enough for my own family. Is it possible here to develop a sense of charity and compassion and extend it beyond the picket fence?

Of course I have changed and of course Australia has too, but really my country and I are not that different. I too want to preserve this lifestyle. I want to keep this sense of space I missed so much; I want to preserve this isolation, this chance for solitude and these occasional silences. I too want a mortgage and a safe, secure life and I don't want to have to face daily poverty, disease and desperation.

But I now feel a conflict in wanting it all. I've realised Australia and I have a childish desire to have it both ways. We want to be part of the world community but at the same time distant and separate. We want the benefits of being an economic player but we don't want to carry the costs. We ignored the Taliban regime's shocking human rights abuses but were loath to accept its most desperate refugees. We were dead keen to join America's war in Iraq but felt fury when those fleeing its consequences floated up on our shores. We jumped keenly into the new war against Afghanistan but were shocked and disbelieving when told this made us a terrorist target.

There's also another change in my country that makes me scared to admit I'm conflicted. It seems Australia has been cheating on me and has been having a love affair with itself while I've been away. And as Australia's selfish streak has developed our modesty has diminished. At first I tried to understand – the Olympic spirit was so sexy I understood the flush of love it sparked. But it seems the affair is turning bitter. It's as if Australia is waking up from an extended one-night stand a little ashamed, a little uglier and badly hung-over and is stumbling to lock the gates, crawl back under the covers and shut its eyes.

When a small article outlining my new feelings about Australia first appeared in the *Sydney Morning Herald* a reader responded with a letter calling me 'sob sister Sarah' and saying if I hated Australia so much I should go back to India. My article hadn't mentioned the word 'hate' once; in fact it was all about love. I was less shocked by the open nastiness of this fellow Australian as by the insecure, angry and emotive nationalism expressed. I'd like to think it was not just fury – perhaps I'd struck a raw nerve of collective guilt, as if I'd exposed that our ideal of 'mateship' was in tatters.

Of course I have no regrets about coming home and my relationship with my country has survived. Australia and I will be together forever and ever. I'll never regret leaving my foster land for my first love and I'll never live anywhere else for long. In fact I'm still celebrating my homecoming with a renewed flush of passion for my country. I'm eating the best fresh food I can find, I'm breathing till my lungs hurt, I sing as I walk in the suburbs and I'm heading for the bush whenever possible. I hope I never take Australia for granted again and I'm still finding it as beautiful as ever.

Yet it's interesting how the places of my childhood seem so much smaller to me now, as does the world we live in. I will always love my land more than any other country on earth. But I don't and won't love it blindly; I'll love it with knowledge of its foibles and problems.

My renewed relationship with Australia is different in other ways as well. We've both changed. While I was thinking Australia was the perfect, ideal nation of free, happy, funny, friendly people with a wonderful empty environment, my country was losing its innocence. And so was I. For I am not much different to my land. We face the same dilemmas. We both have prejudices and problems. We both have to work out how we can be compassionate to strangers while preserving our core values. In an ever-more complex and connected world it's increasingly difficult to know how to behave as nations and individuals. Australia and I need to work out if we can have it all: if we can love without hating others and how we choose to share the love around.

I don't have the answers. I just know that we have to give a little to get something in return. We have to begin to accept that we're part of a global community and we need to know our national character is unique. We should realise that our desire to preserve our isolation, our relative empty landscapes and our high standard of living can look selfish and attracts people who aspire to a life like we lead. We have some decisions to make and I hope we can do it with a sense of duty, compassion and strength. As we discuss and decide I hope we're a little more kind to each other, our country and strangers.

Love is fragile and imperfect but I still believe it will triumph over ignorance and indifference.

Lucy Clark

A print journalist since leaving school, Lucy Clark worked on the *Sun Herald* and the *Daily Mirror* in Sydney before working in the London and New York bureaux of Australian Consolidated Press. Currently she writes a weekly column for Sydney's *Daily Telegraph*. In March this year she attended the Academy Awards on the coat-tails of her Oscar-nominated husband, Guntis Sics. She lives in Sydney with said Nominee and their two children.

LUCY CLARK

Hooray for Hollywood

Oscar Diary
Week one
1 am: Woken by child fluttering eyelids in sleep three rooms away. Sharply aware that Oscar Nominees posted on Web at 12.30 am. Can't sleep – computer right next to bed.

1.01 am: Elbow sleeping possible-Oscar-contender husband in rib. Implore him to drop blasé act and just bloody well log on and find out so we can get back to sleep.

1.01.01 am: Possible Oscar contender logs on in dark and in scary blue light from computer looks like he's about to throw up. Finds Oscar web site and is suddenly bathed in golden light. He grins widely in my direction.

1.01.02 am: Possible Oscar contender becomes official Oscar Nominee for Best Sound, *Moulin Rouge.*

1.02 am: Drop composed adult act and behave like silly children on red cordial. Find that screaming with delight while not waking children much easier than imagined. Marvel that an announcement made in Los Angeles moments earlier can reverberate so wildly in a Sydney suburban bedroom.

1.03 – 7 am: Try to sleep, but toss and turn in knowledge that the apricot water-wave taffeta bridesmaid's dress and white court shoes in box at back of cupboard from 1984 probably won't do for red carpet 2002. Stupid song 'Hooray for Hollywood' repeats on loop in addled brain. V clever Nominee sleeps soundly.

7 am: Sleep at last.

7.10 am: Wake in cold sweat. Scary nightmare about walking up red carpet in orthopaedic house shoes with gnarly unpolished toes – one of them fungal – curling over the front. I'm wearing a threadbare, faded blue towelling ten-year-old house dress with no bra: outline of saggy, uneven, baby-ravaged bosoms v v noticeable. No one is looking at Nicole and everyone is staring at me. Think on reflection that this might not be a bad way to get attention.

7.15 – 8 am: Real life intervenes as children wake and demand breakfast. With talk of Oscar, children think we are discussing neighbour's dog and get v confused. Phone does not stop ringing with congratulations for Nominee, but mainly people wondering what I am going to wear. Children look very perplexed by fact that everyone who is calling today seems to be screaming on other end of line.

8.15 am: Stuck in not-moving-at-ALL Sydney traffic. Disgusted that Oscar Nominee can be treated in this way. Mood improved by prospect of instant fame when radio station rings Nominee on mobile and asks for interview at 8.50 am.

8.16 am: Horror when Nominee realises mobile phone battery is about to go flat and won't be able to do interview while stuck in inside lane of v bad traffic.

8.17 – 8.48 am: Marital joy at international superstardom dissipates v quickly and screaming match about what to do wrecks mood. Sydney traffic v v bad for relationship harmony. Realise only option is to find public phone or make way to nearby aunt's house. Try to ring aunt with news of our impending very important arrival, but phone is engaged. Argue about best shortcut to aunt's house. Nominee decides on the long way.

8.49 am: Screech to a halt outside aunt's house. Appears to be no one home, so break in. Find aunt lolling about on phone in dressing gown. Nominee screams at her to clear the line, put her hands behind her head and lie on floor very quietly. Nominee gaffer-tapes her mouth, rather roughly I think, and waits for radio host to call.

8.50 am: V incisive radio host gets to crux of issue v v quickly and asks Nominee, 'What is your wife going to wear?' Discussions about state of film industry and husband's feelings about being nominated blah blah blah get interviewer off track and just when I think she's going to get back to the main issue, interview is concluded in favour of national news bulletin(!).

9 am: Depart aunt's house to make way to work. Aunt motions to have gaffer tape removed, then asks in a small, disoriented voice from the floor, 'But what are you going to wear?'

9 am – 12 noon: Nominee does back-to-back press

interviews and schedules photographs and TV news for afternoon. I pretend to work but make calls to inform friends and family. Hysterical screaming on end of line alarms nearby colleagues. Walk around in daze. Field persistent questions about what I am going to wear: colleagues I never even talk to, including those with no obvious interest in sartorial splendour, desperate to know what sort of frock I will walk the red carpet in. Total number of frock queries in three hours: thirty-seven.

12.30 pm: Bashing keyboard at desk as though working when superior demands I leave immediately to drink champagne with Nominee.

12.31 pm: Meet Nominee in pub and heart skips a beat with pride when I see how happy he is.

12.35 pm: Crowd turns up to celebrate. Explode myth about Sydney air kissing as two publicists, one actor, one movie producer and one studio executive kiss me on cheek and lips and actually connect with skin. Feel v down-to-earth and special about this.

12.40 – 5 pm: Obscene quantities of champagne quaffed. Publicist realises v quickly that most important issue is what I am going to wear and gets on mobile phone to Famous Fashion Designer and Famous Diamond Designer. Feel like am in an episode of 'Absolutely Fabulous', and head starts to spin.

7 pm: Back at home, Nominee performs household duties with vim while I lie on couch with pillow on head. V v dizzy. Repressed memories of uncontrolled teenage drinking settle unhappily in gullet. Nominee says I must stay upright as am now in training for all-night Oscar bash. Recover just in time to see television footage of us drinking

champagne in pub and feel nauseous again.

7.30 pm: Kiss five-year-old goodnight while holding breath so she doesn't pass out from champagne fumes. She looks pensive and says, 'Everyone seems a bit silly today, don't they Mum?'

7.30.01 pm: I nod in mute agreement, and hum a slow, lullaby version of 'Hooray for Hollywood'.

Week two

Tuesday

10 am: Champagne training has continued all week. Am getting v good. Queries about frock continue too: neighbours, people in the fruit market who have heard the news about Nominee, old friends I haven't heard from in ages. Judging by everyone's reactions and level of interest, going to the Oscars would appear to be modern day equivalent of Cinderella going to the ball. Girlfriends ring up and don't bother with hello, how are you, but spit out, 'Ohmigod what are you going to wear?!?' The question plagues me too, but the action publicist insists Famous Fashion Designer will loan me something. Feel slightly uncomfortable about this, but am consoled by fact that big-name stars – people who actually can afford to spend thousands on a gorgeous frock – get loans for Oscar night. So it's only just and right that a nobody – who would never ever spend thousands on a gown – gets a loan too. Still, am too embarrassed to call Famous Fashion Designer so action publicist arranges for FFD liaison person to call me to set up time for dress-ups. It's true, FFD will gladly loan dress from the archive of catwalk samples. Catwalk model samples? I tell FFD liaison person

that as a 35-year-old mother of two my dimensions are not, ah, exactly what you would find on the catwalks today, and she says, 'You may be surprised.' Mmm, not half as surprised as she's going to be when she sees my Cottontailed bottom struggling its way into those wispy gowns.

Thursday

4 pm: Wear my best clothes to meet liaison person at FFD headquarters. She gives me a quick once-over and goes off to get a selection of gowns and a pair of shoes for height. Am v grateful when she leaves me alone to try on. Most of the dresses don't get past my thighs, and my spirits sink with every stuck zip. FFD liaison person is v encouraging and nice, and keeps bringing in new dresses with determination.

4.30 pm: Finally I find two gowns that fit. FFD liaison person says I can take both home to decide. V v exciting.

6 pm: Try dresses on again at home and flounce around house looking in every mirror at every angle. Discover that it is impossible to sit down in the gorgeous glass-beaded backless number – I can't actually bend in it at all, and in fact it is v uncomfortable and weighs about 30 kilos. Stupidly I still don't rule it out. It's a work of art. The stunning black sequined job is so comfortable and flexible I could cartwheel down the red carpet. This decision would appear to be a no-brainer but naturally I will leave the decision until the last minute and seek as many opinions as possible between now and then.

Week three
Monday

3 pm: Keep looking in the wardrobe at 'the dresses'. Try them on regularly. Friends keep ringing to make appointments to come and see 'the dresses'. Nominee prefers the black sequined job and I secretly agree – it is covered in hand-sewn waves of tiny square silver sequins and has a v sexy split up one leg that goes right up to my post-pregnancy thread veins – but fortuitously stops where my cellulite starts. I think it's the one.

Friday

11 am: Action publicist had made appointment with Famous Diamond Designer. I go to that part of town where normal bank balances fear to tread and am buzzed into the FDD's sparkling salon. I feel like a trespasser in a strange universe and my instinct is to turn around and flee. The prospect of travelling with v v expensive diamonds that don't belong to me freaks me out, but v sweet FDD liaison person puts me at ease immediately. They genuinely want me to enjoy wearing the diamonds and am touched. I have brought the black gown to see what jewels suit, and I put it on. Two FDD women proceed to drape breathtakingly beautiful diamonds on my person. This is real fairytale princess territory, and I'm not ashamed to admit that I am LOVING it.

11.30 am: Diamond choker, diamond earrings and a diamond ring worth a total of $100 000 are chosen. Arrange to pick up on way to airport for flight to LA – do not want those things in my possession a minute more than necessary.

Week four
Monday

10 am: After much soul searching have decided to break a life-long commitment to anti-breast augmentation of any sort and am considering buying my first push-up bra. Chosen dress is v tight and has v gorgeous deep V-neck, and although I thought I would be defiantly proud showing off the real me (saggy, uneven, baby-ravaged bosoms) now decide that a bit of contour and cleavage won't really betray my feminist ideals. Well? If you can't pursue the impossible mammary ideal in Hollywood, then where?

Friday

12 noon: In post champagne-training daze I buy v v expensive shoes I will never wear again, and am now set for LA. Sparkly dress and diamonds: check. Fake bosom shape: check. Painfully high heels that threaten to put back out: check. I simultaneously recognise the sheer silliness of it all, and yet am still so excited. Decide that this is not hypocrisy, merely multifaceted-ness.

Week five
Los Angeles – Oscar Day

6.45 am: Oscar Day dawns cool and grey and way too early. Am too restless and excited to sleep. The last few days have been so long – thought today would never come. Thursday was v glamorous and ended with two swisho cocktail parties where everyone told Nominee he was going to win. This made me v nervous and being v v superstitious spent whole night looking for pieces of wood to touch. Nominee nodded and smiled and looked sanguine, but I know the pressure of expectation is building. Champagne training for the big night v v successful.

6.45 – 9.45 am: Lie awake obsessing over Oscar detail. My stylist (hair and make-up) left a message last night saying she thinks I need mid-brown eyeliner and I only have black. Where's the nearest drugstore? Will it be open? Will I have time to go and get the mid-brown? Will they have mid-brown? What is mid-brown? Will everyone at the Oscars look at me and say ohmigod that woman is wearing black eyeliner, not mid-brown? Nominee snores like a happy labrador next to me while I lie like a horizontal life-sized Oscar (rigid, hands clasped on chest, but not gold). Marvel that he is so relaxed and can actually sleep, but then remember the quantity of champagne Nominee consumed at a v exclusive function yesterday. He was v v excited to see Ron Howard at close range while I was v v excited that my head was at one stage only millimetres from Mel Gibson's bottom (to explain: him standing, me sitting, me resolutely facing away from bottom). Think he may have ruffled my hair with a buttock.

9.46 am: Nominee stirs and we give each other our 'well, this is it' look. It's five weeks since he became a Nominee and we've been on a champagne-fuelled unsustainable high all that time. It's a relief to know we can stop thinking and wondering about it now and just DO it.

10 – 10.30 am: Nominee and I breakfast on our enormous hotel room balcony, which would have a 270-degree view of LA if there were no smog. Through the haze we can see the Hollywood Hills, where the famous HOLLYWOOD sign

looks like messy magnetic letters on a fridge. We get a deep, clenching, abdominal thrill to look at it and know we are here for 'Hollywood's night of nights' and as Rod Stewart would say, tonight's the night.

11 am – 2.30 pm: Stylist turns up to do hair and make-up for me and a fellow nominee's wife, and our hotel room turns into a busy beauty salon. The Nominee is sidelined. Keeps making cracks about it reminding him of his wedding day when, he says, people only knew he was there because he managed to stumble into the photographer's frame a couple of times. Make mental note to discuss this at later date.

2.30 pm: Hair and make-up completed with many congratulations to Jo, who has managed to make us look like a couple of glamours. Slip into my gown while Nominee goes down to the hotel's safety deposit boxes to get the diamonds. My shoulder and arm muscles are still sore from clutching said diamonds to my person on the fourteen-hour flight over here. V nerve-wracking. I put them on and feel like a million, squillion bucks. The irony of the fact that we are here behaving and being treated as though we are rich and famous while we owe about a million, squillion bucks on our house back in Sydney is not lost on me. As ironies go, it's a heavy one.

2.35 – 2.45 pm: Nominee slips into bathroom and emerges tuxed up. I catch my breath and keep it for quite a while. That Armani sure knows how to cut a suit.

2.45 – 3.45 pm: The limo trip through LA is, well, a trip. Anticipation is mounting to almost-screaming point. Our driver, Jerry, tells us this is the lucky car, and that in the twenty-three years he's been driving Nominees to the

Oscars all his passengers have won that little gold statue. The Nominee and I give each other our 'yeah sure, Jerry' look, but secretly hope Jerry is telling the truth and that he is the lucky limo driver.

3.46 pm: A block before the Kodak Theatre in Hollywood we arrive at the security checkpoint. LAPD officers and FBI Bomb Squad dudes in bomb-proof vests swarm the car and check underneath with mirrors. We are waved on towards the theatre and the crowds on the footpath are screaming at the limos and gesturing for us to wind down our windows so they can see who is inside. We don't want to disappoint anyone, so leave the windows up.

3.48 pm: We have arrived. My stomach is full of butter-flies, my chest is full of pride and my head is full of cotton wool. I squeeze the Nominee's knee, kiss him three times for luck, and we give each other our 'let's hold hands while we jump off this cliff' look, and get out of the car.

3.50 pm: We are ushered through a giant tent where there is an enormous security checkpoint through which every-one must pass. My jewels set off the metal detector, but they let me through.

3.55 – 4.15 pm: We emerge from the giant tent onto the famed and long-awaited red carpet. It's like walking out into the Colosseum in its heyday (well, using my imagination here). The roar from both sides of the corridor is over-whelming and deafening. We can't get the grins off our faces. There must be at least 1000 press lined up along the stretch of carpet and they're all yelling out stars' names. Australian media ask Nominee how it feels to be there. Everyone is yelling at the tops of their voices and one can barely be heard, but he tells a microphone boom that it feels like we've all been on a rollercoaster ride and we're just approaching the top of the biggest dipper. We move on, and I mentally finish the rollercoaster analogy: at the end of the ride, someone will be sobbing, someone will be in shock, someone will be vomiting and someone will be screaming with delight.

4.15 – 5 pm: Inside the building we steady our nerves with champagne and meet friends and *Moulin Rouge* colleagues. Nobody, including an old friend, recognises me with make-up on and hair 'done' and they all think the Nominee has brought someone else to the Awards. Stars are absolutely everywhere – it's not so much a matter of star-spotting as normal-person-spotting. Everyone is smaller than you think, except the lead singer from ELO, who has a bigger Afro than I remember. What he's doing here, I can't be sure. Gwyneth Paltrow lopes past me on the stairs, brushing me quite rudely, and Julia Roberts stops short right in front of me to kiss someone and grin that impossibly wide grin. I'm so busy looking at the ELO lead singer's hair and big sunglasses that I miss Sir Paul McCartney and later Sting walking right by me. The Nominee's only stated mission, ever since he was nominated, has been to meet his idol and fellow Nominee McCartney.

5 pm: We are all ordered to our seats in preparation for the live telecast. We walk into the auditorium and on our way to our seat walk past a seated Paul McCartney and Heather Mills. I tell Nominee that this may be his best chance, but he says he can't. We take baby steps forward then the Nominee's and McCartney's eyes miraculously meet. The Nominee seizes the moment and introduces himself as a fellow Nominee and great fan and shakes his

hand. McCartney is v v gracious and smiling, and Nominee tells McCartney that our five-year-old daughter, who has a thing for Beatles' movies and music, wants to marry him when she grows up. McCartney laughs and says in v lovely Liverpudlian accent: 'Tell her I'm taken.'

5.10 pm: Have to push through clutches of air-kissing stars to get to our seats, which are excellent – dead centre eight rows back. In the relatively small crescent of theatre seats in front of us sits Hollywood's who's who, all within spitting distance. It's v fabulous.

5.30 pm: The telecast starts, and the Nominee and I start the nervous, v hard hand squeezing. We are v v nervous, but nevertheless manage to enjoy the ceremony much more than we imagined. Tom Cruise comes on stage and I am sure he keeps looking directly at me. Sandra Bullock, Benicio del Toro, Hugh Jackman, Denzel Washington – I am certain they have all chosen me as their focal point in the audience to keep themselves calm. Is it the sparkling diamonds? The hairdo? After a while I look up, and right above my head is the central camera and autocue. Idiot.

7 pm: After an eternity, it's the last ad break before the Best Sound award. The Nominee and I have squeezed each other's hands into atrophy. My heart is beating so hard I look down and see thousands of silver sequins vibrating in time to my deafening heartbeat. I feel nauseous and dizzy. I want him to win so much because I know how hard he worked and that he deserves it (of course). This is what this whole circus has really been about. If a little fairy had said to me, 'Your husband will win the Oscar, but only if you wear that disgusting drop-waisted apricot water-wave taffeta dress and the white

court shoes from 1984', I know I would have had them out of the back of the cupboard faster than you can say 'Ten Worst Dressed'.

I also know that beyond the nomination, the Oscar recipient is just the lucky one who wins the lottery.

7.05 pm: Halle Berry sweeps on stage to present the Best Sound award. The Nominee and I give each other our brave 'que sera, sera, at least we have each other' look. I've worked out that, when Halle reads out the winners' names, I just have to listen to the first syllable to know if *Moulin Rouge* has won or not. Time stops, but the Nominee's knee does not. He is bouncing it so fast I fear it will come loose at the hip. Halle Berry is ripping open the envelope, I close my eyes and listen for the right syllable, but it's the wrong one, and suddenly someone else is jumping up and down. The Nominee and I do our 'que sera, sera, at least we have each other' look again, this time with a bittersweet twist, and hold hands gently.

7.06 pm: Time slowly winds up again, while our heart rates slow down. *Black Hawk Down won. Black Hawk Down??!! Lord of the Rings, maybe, but Black Hawk Down??!!* I decide to blame pro-military sentiment for this. This is all Osama bin Laden's fault.

7.07 pm: What? Bitter? Moi?

7.08 pm: Disappointment is surprisingly fleeting – am amazed to find we are over it v v quickly and back to soaking it all up, with stupid grins on our faces. The incredible fact that we are here at all obliterates all else.

7.09 – 10.20 pm: The award ceremony, remarkably, continues after Best Sound award. My highlights: Woody Allen, Sydney Poitier, Cirque du Soleil, Ben Stiller and

Owen Wilson – and Jennifer Lopez turning up in apricot water-wave taffeta.

10.30 pm – 12.30 am: The Governor's Ball. Everyone gathers in a sumptuously decorated hall for the US$750-a-head ball where all nominees are supposedly presented with an incredible sample bag of goodies worth $20 000. This turns out to be the biggest myth about the Oscars. Just as the Nominee and I are squabbling over the Tag Heuer watch (well, he has a watch!) we get to the table to find – a set of *postcards* and mini chocolate Oscars which are, admittedly, covered in gold dust. Nominee and I give each other our 'ripped off!' look, shrug, quaff champagne (five weeks of training has paid off beautifully as we can still stand), eat an excellent meal and dance cheek-to-cheek.

1 am: Waiting for one's limo after the Oscars is an equal-ising experience. Everyone, bar no one, has to wait on the freezing sidewalk while three lanes of stretch limos start picking up guests to take them to other parties or, in our case, home to our hotel (in the absence of any invitations to other parties).

1.30 am: Our limo at last. We settle in the back, tell Jerry the driver about his broken run of luck, and give each other our 'that was incredible but we're kind of relieved it's over' look. 'Never,' I say to the Nominee, 'has it been so thrilling to be a loser.' He smiles, nods wearily, and points out the window. As I turn to look, the HOLLYWOOD sign slips out of view.